W9-BVA-861

SURPLUS
DUPLICATE

THE QUESTIONNAIRE

In June 1937, W. H. Auden, Louis Aragon, Stephen Spender and Nancy Cunard circulated a questionnaire to 150 writers in Britain, asking:

"Are you for, or against, the legal Government and the People of Republican Spain?"
"Are you for, or against, Franco and Fascism?"

The answers—mainly for, some against, and a few indifferent to the cause of the Republic—were published in a small book entitled *Authors Take Sides on the Spanish War*. The book was of more than passing interest, as may be seen from the enclosed page comprising excerpts [Appendix III].

It occurred to us that a similar book on the war in Vietnam might prove a useful record of the views of writers—in fact, a cross-section of the intellectual community—at this time. A concern for events in Vietnam is by no means confined to Britain, and we are writing, therefore, to more than three hundred authors in the United States, Britain, France, the Soviet Union, and elsewhere, requesting brief answers to the questions:

Are you for, or against, the intervention of the United States in Vietnam?

How, in your opinion, should the conflict in Vietnam be resolved?

We intend to publish the replies as a small book to appear in the autumn; and would warmly welcome your participation in the questionnaire.

AUTHORS
TAKE
SIDES
ON VIETNAM

Two Questions
on the War in Vietnam
Answered by the Authors
of Several Nations

Edited by

CECIL WOOLF and
JOHN BAGGULEY

SIMON AND SCHUSTER, NEW YORK

ALL RIGHTS RESERVED
INCLUDING THE RIGHT OF REPRODUCTION
IN WHOLE OR IN PART IN ANY FORM
COPYRIGHT © 1967 BY SIMON & SCHUSTER, INC.
PUBLISHED BY SIMON AND SCHUSTER
ROCKEFELLER CENTER, 630 FIFTH AVENUE
NEW YORK, NEW YORK 10020
FIRST PRINTING
LIBRARY OF CONGRESS CATALOG CARD NUMBER: 67–28040
DESIGNED BY CECILE CUTLER
MANUFACTURED IN THE UNITED STATES OF AMERICA

U.S. AIR FORCE

Editors' dedication

To the memory of Nancy Cunard
who conceived and compiled
Authors Take Sides on the Spanish War

Acknowledgments

We have received much help in the preparation of this book. While it would be impractical to name all those in Britain, the United States, and elsewhere to whom we owe thanks for information and advice, it would be invidious not to make mention of the assistance of the following.

We are especially grateful to Ronald Davidson-Houston for translating the contributions from French authors; to Beata Duncan and Lynette Gill for their translations of the German statements; to Angela Faram and Gillian Briggs for their translations of all the Spanish pieces, save that of Camilo José Cela which was translated by Anthony Kerrigan; to Dennis Rhodes, who translated the Italian replies; and Lynette Gill and Sonia Wisniewska for their translations of the two Russian contributions.

We would like to thank Marghanita Laski for the encouragement that she gave at an early stage.

The statement by Norman Mailer is reprinted at his request from *Cannibals and Christians*, Copyright © 1966 by Norman Mailer and reprinted by permission of the author and his agents, Scott Meredith Literary Agency, Inc.

The statement by Lawrence Ferlinghetti "Where is Vietnam?" is Copyright © 1965 by City Lights Books and reprinted at his request from *Where Is Vietnam?* edited by Walter Lowenfels, published by Doubleday & Company, Inc.

The statement by Philip Roth contains the entire text of "Vietcong Village to Be Bulldozed" which appeared in the January 11, 1967, edition of *The New York Times*; the article is Copyright © 1967 by The New York Times Company and reprinted by permission.

Other people have kindly helped us in ways too various to specify. We must content ourselves with naming Roger Bartlett; Léonie Callaghan; James Cracraft; Laurence Czigany; Sarah Dickens; Georgialee Furniss; John Hibberd; Robin and Coral Howells; Stefania Korolczyk; Nicholas Krasso; Judith Millington; Malya Nappi; Brian Pearce; Piers Paul Read; Susan Schneider; Daniel Sperber; James Stegenga; Philip Stewart; Vincent Thompson; Claudio Veliz; Findlay and Jean Wilson and Laurence Zigyn. To all of these, our grateful thanks.

—C.W. & J.B.

Contents

Introduction

This books takes as its inspiration a short collection of writings on the Spanish Civil War published thirty years ago. *Authors Take Sides on the Spanish War* presented the replies to two questions on the war in Spain:

"Are you for, or against, the legal Government and the People of Republican Spain?"

"Are you for, or against, Franco and Fascism?"

The questionnaire was addressed "To the Writers and Poets of England, Scotland, Ireland and Wales"; introduced by a short passage on the irresponsibility of noncommitment, it concluded with the words:

"Writers and Poets, we wish to print your answers. We wish the world to know what you, writers and poets, who are amongst the most sensitive instruments of a nation, feel";

and was signed by Louis Aragon, W. H. Auden, Nancy Cunard, Stephen Spender and other representatives of Western literature.[1]

One hundred and fifty answers, mainly for, some against, and a few indifferent to the cause of the Republic, were published in a small book toward the end of 1937.[2]

The present book is based on a questionnaire of slightly wider scope. It was addressed, not to those living in the British Isles alone, although their replies constitute nearly one half of the collection, but to those read, or widely heard of, in the English-speaking world. This included, at one sweep, scores of writers in the United States, and also—for such is the effect of the translation and the reputation gained at second hand—substantial numbers in Europe and elsewhere.

The questions are as follows:

"Are you for, or against, the intervention of the United States in Vietnam?"

"How, in your opinion, should the conflict in Vietnam be resolved?"[3]

For the phrasing of these questions, the editors have no apologies to make. To some, the word "intervention" may appear to have a moral flavor, derogatory to the United States, but there seems no suitable alternative; "involvement" is inexplicit and "presence" both ingenuous and unhistorical. To others, the second question may appear to lie outside the realm of appropriate debate, the resolution of the conflict too technical a matter for those without admission to the chancelleries of the contending powers; but it is this question which, together with the first, dominates contemporary discussion.

The list of authors to whom this questionnaire was sent is perhaps in greater need of some defense. It was originally intended that the book should be published in Great Britain; in that edition British letters is naturally the most fully represented. But a concern for events in Vietnam is by no means confined to the United Kingdom, and the book was never planned as a purely British undertaking. For the British edition, three hundred authors in the British Isles, half that number in the United States, twenty each in

[1] The full text of the 1937 questionnaire is given in Appendix II, p. 93.

[2] A few of the more interesting answers are to be found in Appendix III, p. 95.

[3] See the frontispiece for the full text of the present questionnaire.

LIBRARY, 620 TCS
APO S. F. 96203

France, the Soviet Union, the two Germanys, Italy, the Spanish-speaking world, and a handful in Eastern Europe, the Middle East, Africa, and Australasia received the questionnaire (or its appropriate translation), principally in the fall of 1966. Of their answers, some 250 are given in the London edition.[4]

The present collection of writings on the war in Vietnam is separate from that impending in Great Britain. The original intention to circulate the questionnaire throughout the English-speaking world, and the attempt to include authors not so favored in the matter of their tongue, render a distinct American edition in part superfluous; nevertheless, the taste and knowledge of the reading public in the United States and Britain, while coextensive, are not identical, and authors appreciated in one hemisphere are not always so regarded in the other. For the American edition, therefore, considerable numbers of replies, from Englishmen and others not widely known in the United States, were deleted from the book, and the attempt was made, with the help of the publishers, to circulate the questionnaire to authors of special interest to American readers and to certain persons who, having earlier received the questionnaire, had not yet seen fit to make reply. Over one hundred extra questionnaires were thus sent out in January 1967.

A generous interpretation was given to "author." Historians, biographers, philosophers, and literary critics, as well as poets, novelists and playwrights, were canvassed for their views; and while their names were chosen in consistent fashion, it was with a consistency that cannot entirely avoid the charge of arbitrary, personal selection. Some were canvassed because the editors felt their works significant, or their answers to the questionnaire potentially of interest; some on the advice of those with special knowledge; some after perusal of the reference books. No one was omitted from the lists on the grounds of his probable political position, nor were any answers, once received, excluded for that reason. A few alterations have indeed been made, none without permission, and generally on grounds of excessive length. Obscurity was not refurbished, nor solecism removed. In this, the editors were guided by Salvador de Madariaga's advice, that "men of letters should have the freedom to bring you their flowers with stems, roots and even some earth attached to them."

The arrangement of the contributions placed the

editors in a difficult position. Whereas the answers to the questionnaire on Spain were divided among three categories, according to whether they were "For," "Against," or "Neutral?" in their judgment of the Republic, no such simple system suggests itself today. A substantial proportion of those responding to the questionnaire offer unequivocal opposition to the intervention of the United States in Vietnam, and a very much smaller number their unhesitating support. Many, however, have taken a less direct approach without necessarily being neutral in their assessment of the war. Themes appear which found no place in 1937. Some attitudes toward the war in Vietnam have been guided principally by the role that that conflict plays in the clash between Great Powers and Ideologies; others by a sense of history; yet more by the complex legal background to the struggle.

In the impending British edition of the present work, six chapters are constructed, according to the themes which have arisen, and the answers are placed within them. Those authors basing themselves on considerations of history, strategy, or law in their attitude toward the war are placed in separate chapters, as are those who more plainly state their position and those who doubt their competence to say anything at all. For the American edition, however, containing only 168 contributions, or two-thirds of the number appearing in the British edition, such classification was held to be redundant, or, to be precise, lacking in that directness with which the American public prefers to be confronted. It is hoped that the classification of authors in the present work according to the alphabet will not prove indigestible, and that the views expressed will not be totally unrelated to those appearing in the larger work and to general literary opinion.

Readers in the United States may be interested to learn of a domestic precedent for the sampling of opinion. Not long after the publication of the 1937 collection of replies on Spain, the League of American Writers set in hand a similar undertaking. Its questionnaire, addressed to the writers of America, called for answers to the same two questions; but, as is not infrequently the case, an idea adopted from elsewhere resulted in a rather more substantial *opus*. A foreword recorded the origins of the notion of questioning authors on the war, mention was made of proceedings and solemn resolutions at various conferences of writers, and, inevitable perhaps in American intellectual life, detailed breakdowns were given of the views of authors in both the United States and Britain. Due deference was paid to scholarship by the addition of appendices and bibliography, while the text of a last-minute telegram from Paris, calling for funds for am-

---

[4] If a comparison is to be made between the nations, it is that the pattern of one third of those canvassed replying to the questionnaire was significantly exceeded only in the case of southeast European, and fallen short of in the case of Soviet, writers.

bulances and signed by Ernest Hemingway, Vincent Sheean and Louis Fischer, lent an air of drama to the undertaking.

Four hundred and eighteen authors responded to the poll conducted by the League. The texts of many of their replies were printed *in extenso;* some were suitably abridged; the receipt of others was acknowledged by printing the author's name alone. Of the contributors to the present book on Vietnam, the reply of Nelson Algren was acknowledged, while the words of Haakon Chevalier, Babette Deutsch, Marianne Moore and Irwin Shaw found greater favor with the editors for the League.

It may not be inappropriate to discuss the purpose of *Authors Take Sides on Vietnam.* The contributors of 1937 and 1938 did not question the significance of what they wrote, and implied, by the scale and confidence of their remarks, that their words might carry weight. The present mood is far removed. The editors were constantly confronted with the notion that writers have no business expressing themselves on matters of politics and world affairs, that their comments are usually ill-informed, their moral censure ineffective. It was even suggested, paraphrasing Ezra Pound, that Vietnam is an emotional luxury to a gang of sap-headed dilettantes. To this position, which has found expression within the answers to the questionnaire, three points may be opposed. First, that writers will set down most cogently the views of artists and intellectuals—if only to express mundane and maudlin sentiment in solid, worthy fashion. Second, that writers, be they ever so remote from practical consideration of war and foreign policy, may—as in regard to Spain—evince a heightened sense of the intransient factors of the time.

The third point concerns present attitudes toward the war in Vietnam. The war has brought a response from writers which has had no precedent in the events of the past twenty-five years. The threat to life and liberty in Hitler's war was perhaps too immediate and all-embracing to permit the outside view, the glimpse of course and consequence; the Cold War's sullen pressures stilled concern and thought in both its camps. But that period is over; and it is with the war in Spain that this issue, in its quickening effect upon opinion, may most readily be compared. The editors hope that this collection will form a part, however modest and insubstantial, of the uncloying of debate.

London, May 1967   *Cecil Woolf and John Bagguley*

An asterisk printed immediately after an author's name indicates that the contribution that follows has been translated.

Nelson Algren

I do not consider the conflict in Vietnam to be an intervention. It is a direct assault, by the American Far Eastern Bomber Command, upon the just aspirations of the peasantry of Southeast Asia. The immediate purpose of this assault is to justify the expenditure of fifty billions of dollars annually in defense: a nation whose economy depends upon such expenditure does not require allies as much as it needs an enemy. The ultimate purpose of this assault is to discover provocation sufficient for bombing the larger Chinese cities; and as the bombing of Nagasaki was an extension of the bombing of Guernica, so will the bombing of China be an extension of the bombing of Japan.

Recent comments by Dwight Eisenhower and Lyndon Johnson sanction such use of the Far Eastern Bomber Command.

"It is a nasty little war but we must win it to survive," Eisenhower explains without explaining what kind of country it is that requires a nasty little war merely to survive.

"Our involvement in Vietnam will never be greater than the Vietnamese people choose to make it," Lyndon Johnson adds. And ever since the people of Santo Domingo pleaded with Mr. Johnson to send in 25,000 marines to restore democracy, we need not be surprised to find that the Vietnamese love us just as much.

Both of these comments reveal that Adolf Hitler's warning—"Those who now most oppose our methods will ultimately adopt them"—is the truest prophecy made in our time.

Yes, I am in full support of bringing Lyndon Johnson to public trial for crimes against humanity. I would not accord such dignity to Hubert Humphrey: I feel that simply putting a pillowcase over his cage would be punishment sufficient.

A. Alvarez

Containment of China should begin in the United Nations from which the USA still debars Peking. These oblique confrontations, savagely involving a third country, are gratuitous, devious, and resolve nothing. The handling is clumsy, the methods brutal, the death-rate unspeakable, the expense disproportionate, and the official figurehead, Ky, ludicrous. I suppose it's good—even essential—for General Motors and the American economy as a whole, but it also alienates everyone, from a significant percentage of the American electorate to the as yet uncommitted nations. As an admirer of America and its realism from way back, I find it odd that a Texan poker player, as shrewd and apparently uninterested in idealism as the President, should be so reluctant to admit the obvious: that the United States is powerful enough not to lose face by negotiating for peace instead of killing for it.

Kingsley Amis

1. Those who favor American withdrawal from Vietnam must either admire communism, or suppose that it is not imperialistic and aggressive, or both. I can do neither. So I support America's present policy.

2. In a peace dictated by America. It may well be impossible to defeat the Communists in the field. Fortunately this is not necessary. They have simply to be convinced that they can never win. They will collapse then.

Hannah Arendt

1. I am against the intervention of the United States in the civil war in Vietnam.

2. The way to resolve an armed conflict is always the same: cease fire—armistice—peace negotiations—and, hopefully, peace treaty.

Giovanni Arpino *

I maintain that the war in Vietnam constitutes an immense shame, a tragic mistake, a grave danger for us, white men. Of what good is it to us to be the heirs of Lincoln and of Churchill, of Roosevelt and of Cavour, of Robespierre and of Pope John XXIII? If we, white men of the present time, do not succeed politically in putting an end to the war in Vietnam, we shall be risking in those marshes, in those thickets, against that people, all the prestige of our culture, all the potentials which our customs, our laws and our traditions still possess.

Unhappily I do not know what to suggest for bringing the conflict to an immediate end: It is for the politicians to take the chestnuts out of the fire, even if it is for the men of culture to enlighten the nations and denounce the inefficiency of the politicians. One thing, however, seems to me certain: It is useless to delude oneself into thinking that the white man can retreat from Vietnam with his prestige intact. This prestige he has already jeopardized by his bombing. Today it is necessary to leave Vietnam even at the cost of giving one cheek to save the other, to save that civilization which is still ours and which we can offer as an example to the young nations. By continuing along this road, by not offering peace to Vietnam, the white man will lose forever the respect of the new nations, and in all corners of the earth he will be looked upon every day as an enemy.

W. H. Auden

1. Why writers should be canvassed for their opinion on controversial political issues, I cannot imagine. Their views have no more authority than those of any reasonably well-educated citizen. Indeed, when read in bulk, the statements made by writers, including the greatest, would seem to indicate that literary talent and political common sense are rarely found together.

2. If, as a social human being, I am asked my opinion about some political issue in England, Europe, or the United States, my answer, however stupid or prejudiced, is at least in part based upon personal knowledge. I have traveled in the countries concerned, I know something about their inhabitants, their history, their language, their ways of thinking. But what do I, or any other writer in the West, know about Vietnam, except what we can glean from the newspapers and a few hurriedly written books? We know far more, even, about China.

3. It goes without saying that war is an atrocious corrupting business, but it is dishonest of those who demand the immediate withdrawal of all American troops to pretend that their motives are purely humanitarian. They believe, rightly or wrongly, that it would be better if the Communists won.

4. My answer to your question is, I suppose, that I believe a negotiated peace, to which the Vietcong will have to be a party, to be possible, but not yet, and that, therefore, American troops, alas, must stay in Vietnam until it is. But it would be absurd to call this answer *mine*. It simply means that I am an American citizen who reads *The New York Times*.

A. J. Ayer

I find the first of your questions easier to answer than the second. I do not think that the United States should have gone to war in Vietnam, and I do not think that its conduct of the war is either morally justifiable or even defensible on grounds of expediency.

It is, however, not at all clear to me how the conflict should now be resolved. Certainly the United States Government should declare its willingness to negotiate not only with the Government of North Vietnam but also with the Vietcong, with a view to the holding of elections throughout Vietnam under international supervision. The difficulty is that it is far from certain that the North Vietnamese Government would agree to negotiate unless the Americans first withdrew their troops. I think that the United States should accept this condition, but do not think it at all probable that it will. If it is not politically possible for it to go so far as this, I think that it should at least call a halt to its offensive operations, and confine the activities of its troops to holding certain bases. There is some chance that this would lead to a stalemate out of which negotiations could arise.

James Baldwin

I am against United States intervention in Vietnam on moral grounds because it is wrong; on political grounds because we are deluded in supposing that we have the right or the power to dictate the principles under which another people should live.

It would seem to me that our presence in Vietnam is a direct result of the parochial and political attitudes of the United States Government for the last two decades, at least.

The conflict cannot possibly be resolved as long as our military presence there is so devastating. It would seem to me that the first step would be for the United States to abandon its policy of conversion by fire and permit the problem to be brought before the United Nations.

George Barker

Goddammit, every US bomb dropped on Hanoi canstitoots a triumph of the American Way of Life. For chrissakes, whaddya want us to drop? Billy Graham?

Vernon Bartlett

I am against American intervention in Vietnam, although not necessarily for the reasons expressed by many others who are also against it. My reasons are these. I believe that the war there, if prolonged, will end either in increasing humiliation for the United States or in another world war arising from the desire to avoid that humiliation. I need not write of the appalling disaster that another world war would represent, but a few words about the alternative—humiliation for the Americans—are necessary. I do not believe it would be a good thing for the world as a whole if the United States were to return to that isolation for which we used to condemn her. I loathe many of the activities of the CIA. I am constantly infuriated by the disastrous idea that what is good for Americans (or is presumed by Madison Avenue to be good for them) is also good for the rest of the world. But I do not forget the generous intentions of masses of ordinary Americans, as expressed through the United Nations, the efforts to relieve famine, and so on. The world would not be the gainer if a people industrially so powerful and basically so decent were to become embittered.

As I see it, the danger the Americans now face is less that the Chinese may become militarily more active than that the South Vietnamese will become actively hostile. Is it logical to expect that the Vietnamese peasant will indefinitely accept the theory that these large, strange, pink men from the other side of the world, who drop napalm bombs on his village and burn his crops and his forests, are his friends, and that other Vietnamese, whose language and customs he can understand, are his enemies? Is it not probable that communism is a creed which he, with no experience of self-government, can better understand than democracy?

It may be that Communist reprisals are more deliberately cruel than those of the South Vietnamese and the Americans—in the course of more than forty years of journalism, I have learned to pay very little attention to stories of atrocities or to estimates of casualties —but the discrepancy in the armaments means that American destruction is on a much greater scale. In one case, two or three people in a village are put to death very cruelly in order to intimidate other potential informers; in the other, the whole village is bombed to hell.

President Johnson has declared time after time that all he wants is to assure for South Vietnam a democratic Government. But genuinely democratic elections might quite possibly produce a Communist victory. What then? I fear that the White House has for too long (and not only in Vietnam) depended upon local leaders who have no more confidence in democracy than I have in the Flat Earthers. The Communists in Malaya were defeated only when a Malayan Government had taken over control from the British. Tunku Abdul Rahman had far more popular support than any leader in Vietnam has been able to enlist. The elections held in September 1966 seem to have been a step in the right direction, despite the campaign for mass abstentions. But one would have far more hope of a peaceful settlement if it were made clear that the Vietcong representatives had a full right to sit at any conference table.

Perhaps my principal reason for criticizing the American intervention is that the ideas of an immensely rich and industralized country are utterly unsuited to the countries of Southeast Asia—countries which are financially poor but which have old civilizations worthy of respect and admiration. Much about the British government of underdeveloped nations was valuable, but I believe the doctrine that democracy was necessarily to be expressed by one-man-one-vote has been disastrous—there could be no surer way of replacing government with some traditions behind it by government by demagogues with none. Much about the

American help to underdeveloped countries is valuable, but the belief that the American way of life in every way marks an advance on the way of life of other peoples is, in my opinion, utterly disastrous.

How should the Vietnam conflict be resolved? By admission of China to the United Nations—if, indeed, she can be persuaded by her friends to seek admission. By frank admission that "democracy" in Vietnam or anywhere else must be accepted even if it produces a predominantly Communist Government. By the limitation of American activity, until negotiations can be arranged, to holding certain strongpoints in South Vietnam—complete and unconditional withdrawal would doubtless be more satisfactory to those of us who see the danger of another world war, but there is a limit beyond which a people's national pride will not go. By a refusal to encourage attempts at mediation by India and other countries whose Governments could not, by any stretch of imagination, be looked upon as impartial in the present Sino-American dispute. And by a tremendous campaign in the United States to remind the people that the trouble in Vietnam is infinitely less important than the attempt to arrive at reasonable relations with Russia and China, which is out of the question as long as the Vietnam dispute endures.

Simone de Beauvoir *

In a word: I am absolutely against the intervention of the United States in Vietnam.

The conflict should be resolved by the evacuation of the American forces. Furthermore, Johnson is in my opinion a war criminal quite as guilty as those who were condemned at Nuremberg.

S. N. Behrman

I execrate our war in Vietnam and the fomentors of it. It is, as Fouché said of the murder of the Duc d'Enghien, worse than a crime. It is a blunder. I share the feeling of a Professor of Physics in the University of Rochester who wrote a letter to *The New York Times* a year ago. He said that what we are doing in Vietnam makes him ashamed to be American. I endorse the statement recently issued by Thomas Boylston Adams of Massachusetts. He said: "By guile and by subterfuge the President has carried the nation into war without consent of Congress or debate in the Senate."

I believe that the conflict in Vietnam should be resolved by our withdrawal. *The New York Times,* which has been critical of the war, says that this is impossible; we would lose "face," the confidence of the Asian peoples, etc., etc. I agree with the statement made by de Gaulle in Cambodia recently in which he draws the analogy of the French withdrawal from Algeria. Neither he nor France lost face by it. Our withdrawal could be phased. Sanctuary could be provided in enclaves protected by our troops for those endangered by reprisal. This war is a sin to high Heaven. A great leader would acknowledge it and liquidate it and would, I believe, by doing so, win the grateful plaudits of the world.

Nathaniel Benchley

I am against the intervention of the United States in Vietnam, because I don't think our interests are sufficiently involved to warrant all the effort—or, if they are, nobody has made it clear as to why they are, and

God alone knows how the conflict should be resolved. I don't think heightening the military effort is the answer, because that is trying to impose a military solution to a nonmilitary question, but after all this hoo-rah we can't just turn around and run. The whole thing should have been debated in 1954, not now.

I think the President has listened to the admirals and generals, rather than to his own heart.

Isaiah Berlin

I am still quite clear about what I felt in the middle thirties—I was wholly pro-Spanish Republican, and remain so still. I wish I could be equally clear about Vietnam. I do not know how that war is to be ended. I think it was probably a terrible mistake on the part of the Americans to have sent troops there in the first place. I wish the Vietnamese had originally been left to settle the issue by and for themselves; unlike the Spanish situation, Vietnam seems to me to have called for genuine nonintervention. But I do not wish American withdrawal now to lead to—as it well might—a massacre of those who are or might be found (rightly or wrongly) to be American allies. It is frightful that Vietnamese villages should be bombed and the innocent continuously killed. But it seems to me even more dreadful to abandon people to massacre by their enemies. How is one to guarantee that this will not happen? Or that a precipitate and total American withdrawal would not cause other Southeast Asian Governments to be intimidated into knuckling under to regimes which many of their citizens would surely hate? We are often told that their existing regimes are no better and no more popular than any communist regime would be; but I am not convinced of this. To put people in a situation where they lose their liberty or change Governments under alien pressure, because they are convinced that nobody will help them—to create a kind of terrorized joining of the bandwagon like that which took place in Central Europe in the last years of the 1930's—is something that no decent person could want. I do not know whether this parallel is valid; but I need convincing that it is not. I simply do not know enough about the situation in Vietnam to know whether the various courses advocated by, say, Walter Lippmann, or Senator Fulbright, or Professor Arthur Schlesinger, Jr.—phased withdrawal for instance, or enclaves, and the like—are feasible. If such courses as these are likely to prevent the two prospects that I have mentioned, and which it seems to me to be morally indefensible for us to urge, I should be very strongly indeed for them. But I do not know how practicable such a policy in fact would be. Still, even so, if I had to vote, I should vote for it.

Thus, I find myself in the unsatisfactory position of having to qualify my answer. I wish I could answer boldly and clearly, as most of my friends seem able to do, with an unconditional yes or no. In the Spanish question I felt, whether rightly or wrongly, no doubts at all. I feel none about the policies of South Africa, Rhodesia, Spain, Portugal; or about Budapest in 1956. I felt clear about the Korean War—the United Nations seem to me to have acted rightly. I envy those who feel as certain about Vietnam. The Americans have a bear by the tail, and their position is unenviable; and that, quite apart from the question of prestige and the balance of world power; yet withdrawal without a negotiated settlement could lead to even more cruelty and suffering than that which it is intended to end. I am for whatever solution is likely to cause least destruction and oppression. I am not for a *ruat coelum* stand on some absolute principle: least of all for an ideological crusade, or arrogant or simpleminded insistence on importing our own methods or institutions into countries which have their own, perhaps quite different, traditions and aspirations. I am only too well aware that this is not a very clear-cut answer to your question. But I feel sure that I am not alone in experiencing the perplexities which I have done my best to describe.

After these perplexities and qualifications, which remain with me, let me add this: Apart from the small group who appear to share my doubts, I cannot help finding myself far closer to those who wish the war stopped at any price than to their adversaries. If I had to choose between the two extremes, I have no doubt which I should choose.

Giuseppe Berto *

The politicians of my country, Italy, waste a considerable amount of the time which they could more usefully dedicate to the grave problems that afflict us, by making interminable speeches on the war in Vietnam, about which they obviously know little and on which they give conflicting opinions, following the points of view of the party to which they belong. I myself, with regard to such a painful and troublesome affair, have only this to say: *I am very sorry about it.*

Mongo Beti *

Naturally, as a Negro, I disapprove entirely of the American presence in Vietnam, since its aim is plainly the perpetuation of an odious and intolerable order, by attempting to check with bombs a process of social and political change desired by the majority of the South Vietnamese people. To my mind the present situation glaringly illustrates the reactionary role which the Americans are playing in the world, just as could be seen not so long ago in the Congo. To what avail is indignation when the poor and oppressed, searching for the future, find inspiration in Marxism? Should one not rather deplore the fact that Christianity has abdicated its original claim of justice and brotherhood?

Peace negotiations must be opened, the Americans having previously undertaken, as the French President has proposed, to send home their forces within a reasonable time.

Edmund Blunden

My views are simple: I am against the intervention of the US in Vietnam; and the conflict should be resolved by the withdrawal of their troops—the sooner the better.

Hector Bolitho

My answers to your questions depend upon what I feel rather than what I know, of the complicated political reasons behind the tragedy of Vietnam. I know only what the newspapers tell me. I am a pacifist and I suppose that this guides my opinions of all wars. Why a political leader of any country should have the power to order thousands of "the young, all unfilled" to sail to their death is beyond me. The political leader who signs a Declaration of War should, by international agreement, be the first man shot. This might stay his pen.

There is another point that occurs to me. I am not a flag-waving Briton. I was born in New Zealand and I still have a New Zealand passport. We are quietly drifting away from Britain because of necessity, but I believe the Briton was good for most of the countries he governed. Especially in Africa. The moment he withdrew, the natives enjoyed their frontiers and divided themselves to fight across them. A backward trend. The politician who creates a frontier creates a battlefield.

This may seem to be an evasion of your question, but it is the reason why I hate all wars; the reason why I hate the American intervention in Vietnam.

You ask "how" in my opinion "should the conflict be resolved." Frankly, I think it is too late to do this peacefully. American statesmen are ignoring the lessons of history and of human behavior. They put their pride first, just as we did when we went out and killed our kind during the American War of Independence. They are repeating the oldest mistake of history, by sending the young to die in Vietnam. "Theirs not to reason why, Theirs but to do and die" are pretty near the most disgusting lines in English poetry.

Heinrich Böll *

Of course I am unreservedly against US intervention in Vietnam, but thinking about a solution fills me with trepidation, because the situation is tangled and confused. It seems to me that the neutral powers, among which I would include France, should again and again ask the Soviet Union also to mediate in this affair. This may be very foolish, but it appears to me as the only possibility, since I think it important to protect the interests of Vietnam against the two interested parties, China and America. Another possibility would be an appeal by the Pope to the Catholics in Vietnam to make and keep the peace. Since in Vietnam it seems also (or even primarily) to be a question of economic

systems or principles, the Pope would have to say something fundamental to his Catholics there about the *theology of private property* and the *theology of exploitation*. If the Soviet Union and the Pope—and this combination does not seem altogether Utopian to me—could be persuaded, there might be some hope of *peace* in Vietnam.

Robert Bolt

I do not know exactly how and when the war in Vietnam started. Each side accuses the other of having first disturbed the *status quo*, ascribing to itself a merely defensive reaction. The interesting question anyhow is not what "incidents" came first but by what agency such obscure origins could grow to such a monstrous conflict. And the eager reciprocity of both sides is the answer, their continuing determination to give better than they get.

The result of this process is intolerable for two reasons: Firstly, the war is being fought by criminal means. Secondly, it is being fought without consulting the wishes of the South Vietnamese people, who mainly suffer and whose interests both sides claim to champion.

Now as to the criminal means: South Vietnamese forces interrogate by torture. This is admitted in our national press, sometimes with accompanying photographs. I do not know that the Americans themselves interrogate by torture, but the South Vietnamese Government derives its power from American aid and the Americans must take responsibility for the use to which that power is put. We must indeed assume that they approve it while that aid continues and increases. The Vietcong also use torture and I equally condemn them for it. But I am committed by my Government to the support of the Americans and their allies, so that their actions concern me more particularly.

The use of frightful and indiscriminate weapons against civilian or only partly military targets is criminal. Napalm and "lazy dogs" are such weapons and are so used, alas, by the Americans themselves. The enemy would doubtless use them similarly if he had them but happily for him he hasn't. The Americans alone must bear the guilt of this.

This general and seemingly accepted practice of frightfulness is my first reason for opposing the continuation of the war and for condemning particularly the American part in it. No political ends justify criminal means. My second reason concerns those ends themselves.

South Vietnam is now in three parts: the area under American control, the disputed area, and the area controlled by the Vietcong.

In the area under American control, and despite the authoritarian Governments which they have sponsored, there have been vigorous protests from substantial sections of the population. American bases are subject to daring if ferocious acts of sabotage. I give no more credence to the results of the elections there than I would to elections held in their part of Vietnam by the Vietcong.

In the disputed area, the military situation is arrived at on the American side by sheer weight of metal, on the enemy side by the operation of guerrilla armies living largely off the land. Such armies cannot operate without at least the acquiescence of the sitting population. The Vietcong policy of redistributing large land-holdings sufficiently explains the goodwill of the poorer peasants. It also suggests opposition from less numerous classes. I do not doubt that terror is resorted to where good will is lacking, but don't believe that terror can suffice. If terror could suffice, presumably the South Vietnamese forces could operate similarly. It was their inability to do so which called forth such massive and sophisticated military aid from the Americans.

In the area under Vietcong control, through which pass the attenuated supply lines from the North, we hear of no popular resistance. If there were such resistance, the Americans would have made it known. Its absence, in an area of jungle villages impossible to police, argues again acquiescence or good will.

Against all this I remember that the Vietcong and the North Vietnamese are armed by China and must to some extent be China's creatures and be known to be. But this applies with double force to the Americans who are in person plainly foreigners in Vietnam.

In short, I accept with material reservations the Vietcong claim to be the champions of the people; the American claim I reject. I believe that they are in Vietnam for no other purpose than to prosecute their general crusade against communism wherever it appears. The wishes of the people do not seriously concern them. Nor, to do them justice, do they very seriously pretend it. Their final argument is not that they must stay in South Vietnam because the people want them to; their final argument is just that communism must be held in South Vietnam or elsewhere—so it might as well be there.

As to how the war might be concluded: Ideally both sides would withdraw their forces and agree to stand by the results of genuinely popular elections which would be conducted by some neutral agency to find out what support there really is for Marshal Ky, the Vietcong, and anybody else who offered. But the ideal is not to be expected. So long as either side believes that it can win the war the best we can expect is military exhaustion, the military substitute for common sense. The worst we have to fear is a steady growth of conflict with the possibility of nuclear Armageddon at the end of it.

Between the ideal and the expected is the middle ground of reasonable hope. Like the Americans I am hostile to and frightened of communism. Unlike them (apparently) I do believe what they say: that people don't go Communist if they can see a decent alternative. It is too late now for the Americans to show that alternative to the people of South Vietnam. There they face the usual confused but invincible mixture of patriotism, xenophobia and popular desire for betterment, led—as always where more moderate leadership has been repressed—by the Communists. My hope is that the Americans will make what terms they can, withdraw from Vietnam, and then by massive aid and education offer the decent alternative to other countries which are in similar straits but still hang on to democratic aspirations. India would seem to be a splendid and politically crucial field for it. This method of resisting communism would be better in itself than war but also more effective. However it would ask of the Americans not only their old generosity and courage but a new open-mindedness. My hope is reasonable but not strong.

Kay Boyle

There are entire days of anguish, and entire nights without sleep, when there seem to be no words left to condemn the horror of our actions in Vietnam. But if one's own vocabulary fails, then one must use the words of American professors, of American churchmen, and of the men in our Government, who speak out with courage and logic, and without hypocrisy. There are the words of Professor Staughton Lynd, for instance, which declare that if President Johnson really wanted to discuss peace in Vietnam, he could do so from the White House merely by picking up the telephone. Professor Lynd placed a call after breakfast one morning to the National Liberation Front headquarters in Prague. Within an hour and a half, he was in conversation with a representative of the NLF who spoke fluent English. "I am not so simpleminded," Lynd has said, "as to suppose that wars can be ended by after-breakfast telephone calls. But somehow, somewhere, there must be a beginning of a dialogue with our antagonist. Therefore, I ask in all seriousness if President Johnson has the right to continue the escalation of the terrible mutual slaughter in Vietnam until he has picked up the phone."

Or one can use the words of Father Philip Berrigan. He has said that our indiscriminate attacks with bombs and napalm against innocent peasants in the hope of rooting out a few Vietcong, our plans to bomb the dikes of North Vietnam, an act which would result in the drowning of perhaps hundreds of thousands of Vietnamese—indeed, the whole rising tide of savagery and ruin which we have brought into being—these outrages contradict the Gospel and make fidelity to it a mockery. Then let us once and for all, Father Berrigan says, renounce Christianity honestly and openly as being incompatible with our present policy in Southeast Asia.

Or listen to Senator Fulbright, now chairman of the Senate Foreign Relations Committee. He says that the campuses of our universities are inhabited by institutes and centers with awe-inspiring names, which use vast Government funds to produce ponderous studies of insurgency and counter-insurgency—studies which look suspiciously like efforts to develop scientific techniques for the prevention of revolutions, without regard for the possibility that some revolutions may be justified or even necessary. "We are rich and satisfied in a world of desperate poverty and human degradation," Fulbright says, "and we delude ourselves if we suppose that the forces of change in the emerging nations are likely to be consummated everywhere without violence and profound social dislocation. . . . Whether our own domestic values are to be conserved in the world or are to be swept away in a tide of violent upheaval is likely to be determined by America's ability and willingness to support social revolution." It is not an easy thing for a nation like the United States to associate itself with revolutionary change, Fulbright has warned, but he believes that the future of the world may depend upon our being able to do so.

Or hear George Kennan saying on the question of Vietnam: "I would submit that there is more respect to be won in the opinion of this world by a resolute and courageous liquidation of unsound positions than by the most stubborn pursuit of extravagant or unpromising objectives. I cannot imagine that anyone with any degree of responsible concern for the fortunes of the people of this country could ever have given to any foreign political authority an unlimited commitment on our resources and on our manpower. I

just do not see how this is conceivable. I would fight with every fiber of my being against the suggestion that we should ever give to any foreign political authority anything in the nature of an *indefinite* commitment on the resources of America."

As for my own words about our intervention in Vietnam, I stand helpless and appalled before the most shameful page and the most concerted record of immorality in American history. As a first step toward the resolution of that conflict, I would recommend that President Johnson take the only dramatic political action possible at this late date: that he go immediately to Vietnam and have a personal confrontation with the leaders of the National Liberation Front.

John Braine

As long as the United States is in Vietnam, Australia and New Zealand are safe. And in South Vietnam at least there is some semblance of freedom, some hope, however faint, of a better future.

The war must be ended by negotiation; it is hardly possible that it can be ended by military defeat. The ensuing peace will depend entirely upon the United States continuing to maintain a military establishment in Vietnam.

The course is not between right and wrong but between a number of courses, all of which will entail great suffering. The President's task is to decide which course entails the least suffering and at the same time best serves the interests of his own country. I suggest, incidentally, that the interests of the United States are far more likely to coincide with the interests of Great Britain than with those of the Vietcong or Communist China.

John Malcolm Brinnin

1. With chilled resignation and embarrassed cynicism, I have learned to live with outrage from day to day; but I am undermined by an endless sense of shame. The intervention of the United States in Vietnam has been, for me, the source of a relentless, nagging awareness of spiritual attrition next to despair. By silent consensus and callous default, we have permitted our Government to wage an undeclared war and thus to shrink our pretensions of decency and honor to images of smiling arrogance. In the exercise of our power, it seems to me, we have betrayed our strength.

2. I have no ideas about ways in which the conflict should be resolved, but I am certain that no lasting resolution will be effected without our first achieving a vigorous restatement of identity and purpose. If we are going to police the world, then we are going to have to accept the fact that we will brutalize ourselves as well as those whom we choose to protect. If we are going to lead the world, we shall do so by the example of our domestic history and by an absolute restraint upon actions that may even remotely seem like reassertions of imperial prerogative. Without such a restatement we will continue to be in thrall to tribal minds—minds that cannot operate beyond the archaic demands of militarism and the suicidal gambits of diplomacy.

Vera Brittain

As one of the authors invited in 1937 to answer the questionnaire on the Spanish War, I replied:

> I hold war to be a crime against humanity, whoever fights it and against whomever it is fought. . . . I detest Fascism and all that it stands for, but I do not believe that we shall destroy it by fighting it. And I do not feel that we serve either the Spanish people or the cause of civilization by continuing to make Spain the battleground for a new series of Wars of Religion.

This reply was, for some reason best known to the editors, classified as "neutral?" Clearly it did not take the extreme political position desired by those who sent out the questions.

The experiences of the past thirty years have not caused me to alter my view, but the position of Vietnam, though not dissimilar from that of Spain in 1937, is not identical. I note your interest in obtaining the views of an authentic cross-section of "the intellectual community." To my unshaken conviction that war is a crime against humanity in all circumstances, I would therefore add the following brief modifications:

1. I am against the exploitation of small countries by great powers, whether the United States, Britain, Russia or any other.

2. The conflict in Vietnam should therefore be resolved through an international agency such as the United Nations. I am aware that the power of the UN is less direct, and therefore less immediately effective, than that of a strongly armed state, but it has the con-

science of the world behind it, and the authority of conscience, in the short run as in the long, remains as indestructible as that of the Crucifixion.

Brigid Brophy

I am naturally against the United States' war in Vietnam; I am against any power which marches into a foreign country, occupies half of it and, using that half as a base, bombs the other. However, anyone who values his freedom to express his opinions as I am doing at this moment is bound to feel qualms about abandoning South Vietnam to a Communist fate. If the American qualms are on that score, they are honorable but unrealistic. The only choice the Americans can at present (July 1966) offer the South Vietnamese is not between communism and freedom but between communism and military occupation, plus a propped-up regime (the elections scheduled for 1956 have still not taken place) and a strong chance of getting killed either by the Communists on purpose or by the Americans accidentally. The longer this continues the more the South Vietnamese will conclude, correctly, that communism is by far the less dire alternative. As for the North Vietnamese and the Vietcong, bombing them may convert some of them into dead or mutilated Communists but it will not convert a single one, as the Americans unimaginatively expect it to do, into an anti-Communist. It will merely turn the convinced Communists among them into embittered, ruthless and brutal Communists, and turn the indifferent among them rabidly anti-American.

The obvious way out is to rely on the 1954 Geneva Agreements. Unfortunately, this is an obviously inadequate way out, as it is the one point on which the United States, North Vietnam and the Vietcong all agree and yet they are all still fighting. North Vietnam insists the Americans honor the Geneva provision that Vietnam should be free of foreign troops. The Americans suspect that, if they did, the Communists would either ignore any provision that might be made for free elections in Vietnam or, which from the American point of view would be worse, win them. The North Vietnamese have a sound legalistic point and the Americans a sound political one—for, while there is no truth in the American article of faith that no one ever votes Communist with his eyes open and being in his right mind, it is true that if a people once votes Communist in its right mind and then changes its mind, it seldom gets a chance to vote non-Communist next time.

Since we are in a politico-legalistic impasse, the politicians should perhaps stop going through the conventional routines of power politics, which in the past 3,000 years have so regularly led us to conferences that break down and thence to war. Why not an imaginative act which would simply tunnel beneath the legalisms and the qualms? Why shouldn't the Americans get out of Vietnam, taking with them any Vietnamese who want to go? It happens that the two powers who are actually fighting on the American side in Vietnam, namely Australia and New Zealand, and one of the powers on the International Control Commission set up by the 1954 Geneva Conference, namely Canada, are underpopulated and given to advertising for emigrants. Let them offer citizenship to any Vietnamese who want it. (Australia would, of course, have to abrogate its "white Australia" policy—a step which in itself would be an enormous contribution to world good will, would win millions of Asiatic hearts away from incipient communism and would surely be preferable, even in Australian eyes, to the deaths of white Australian soldiers in Vietnam.) If you are going to intervene in another country's affairs on the grounds that you feel them as keenly as you do your own, the only way to justify yourself and attest your sincerity is to be prepared to receive its citizens as your own.

To shift and resettle a good part of the population of Vietnam (always supposing the Vietnamese did not prefer en masse to stay in a Communist Vietnam, in which case the American conscience would be freed honorably and cheaply) would of course be a fantastic operation on an almost inconceivable scale. I surmise it would cost an infinitesimal part of what it cost, reckoned in money alone and with pain and grief left out of the account, to keep up the war.

Robert Brustein

1. I am unequivocally opposed to the United States intervention in Vietnam, shamed by the brutal expression it leaves upon the face of my nation, and comforted only by the thought that, unlike the Germans, Americans have not been completely supine before the squalid decisions of their leaders.

2. Immediate withdrawal of all our forces is the only action morally adequate to the occasion, but since this might be interpreted as weakness by the more belligerent Communist nations and lead to unwanted infiltration in other unprotected areas, the more practical alternatives would be to (1) halt the bombings in the North, and (2) hold purely defensive positions in the South until an international tribunal can arbitrate the differences between the Southern Government and the Vietcong. I would hope that the United States would volunteer indemnities to all the victims of this war, including the families of its own soldiers, as an initial step toward asking forgiveness of history.

William F. Buckley, Jr.

I am in favor of it. America's commitment is to a beleaguered people. It is a commitment originally made by a man who knew a great deal about dying, and about war making, and about war prevention, that having been Eisenhower's professional training and professional concern back when he swore, with the backing of the people's representatives, to defend Southeast Asia against the Communists. That pledge was reaffirmed by his successor, who knew war from the heroic isolation of a long night in the Pacific Ocean spent retrieving the broken bodies of companions who had gone down under enemy fire. That pledge has been reaffirmed, once again, by Lyndon Johnson. As a Christian, I consider it fantastic to urge acquiescence in a Communist takeover, or on grounds of "conscience" to commend an entire population to the superintendence of the Vietcong.

What are we doing in South Vietnam, if not trying to save Southeast Asia from the Communists? Yet if this is our purpose, how long can we put off facing the strategic realities? That situation is simply this, that we cannot keep South Vietnam free without taking action against North Vietnam, whose capacity to extravasate terrorists into Free Vietnam is beyond our capacity, or the free Vietnamese's, to cope with. It is all very well for us to distribute literature to South Vietnamese hamlets about the glories of democratic government. It is something else to reply persuasively to the arguments used by the Vietcong Communist guerrillas. Their favorite form of cajolery is to descend on pro-Western hamlets, pick out the leaders, and publicly disembowel them. The effect on putative freedom lovers is said to be considerable. How can we hope, under the circumstances, to have the people of South Vietnam with us? Why should they be "with us" when we permit our fear of world opinion to count more heavily than their fear of the Vietcong guerrillas with their bloody pangas?

What the President needs is a first-class balky Congress, a Congress of dug-in naysayers, who will by gawd wrest information from Mr. Johnson about matters of public concern, or refuse to continue blank-checking him along his tortured odysseys. It is not merely to play politics to demand from a Chief Executive in a mature democracy the right to participate in the decision-making.

LBJ has not yet told Congress, or the people: a) Why do we not encourage the use of Asians in the battlefield? b) How can we hope to win an enduring peace so long as the Red Chinese are left free to continue to develop their atom bombs?

America's primary responsibility is, surely, to supply what preeminently it is in a position to supply, namely, the materiel of war. That and, most important of all, the ultimate resolution, which is our determination to use our total resources if necessary in order to protect the freedom fighters there. In a word, to provide the South Vietnamese with the shelter of our nuclear umbrella.

Initial steps should be taken, leading, ideally, to the day when the American presence in South Vietnam would be purely advisory and logistical: and when the peoples of Free Asia could join hands together, as was done so often by the peoples of Europe, to repel the common oppressor.

James Burnham

I am for the intervention of the United States in Vietnam because I do Lenin, Stalin, Brezhnev, Mao Tsetung and Lin Piao the honor of taking them seriously. *Mao:* "The seizure of power by armed force, the settlement of the issue by war, is the central task and the highest form of revolution. This Marxist-Leninist principle holds good universally." *Lin:* "Taking the entire globe, if North America and Western Europe can be called 'the cities of the world,' then Asia, Africa and Latin America constitute 'the rural areas of the world.' Since World War II, the proletarian revolutionary movement has for various reasons been temporarily held back in the North American and Western European capitalist countries, while the people's revolutionary movement in Asia, Africa and Latin America has been growing vigorously. In a sense, the contemporary world revolution also presents a picture of the encirclement of cities by the rural areas."

I believe the conflict in Vietnam should be resolved by the defeat of the Communist-led armed force as a necessary action in the protracted conflict to counter the advance of "the contemporary world revolution."

William S. Burroughs

I don't as a rule interfere in political matters once a problem has reached the political-military stage it is already insoluble. However I sometimes think out loud: the French were in Indochina if my memory serves quite some years before they found out they were losing at any exchange rate of casualties . . . losing their professional soldiers and they found out again in Algiers. Now you take a formula like Nationalism=Army Police=trouble with other Stone Age tribes . . . and when they start using atomic bombs instead of stone axes=closing time, gentlemen. Well looks like some folks figure the only solution to this mess is blow up the set and start over may have happened several times already the species being about five hundred thousand years old and what we call history dating back only ten thousand years give a little take a little what were they doing for four hundred and ninety thousand years? Now if you *dont* want to see the whole set go up of course the Americans should get out of Vietnam before: "American and Chinese troops clash north of Hanoi" . . . "Johnson in the toughest speech yet" . . . "Kosygin bluntly warned" . . . And of course every nation should destroy their atomic weapons and maybe their atomic physicists as well to make sure but even that would pose quite a disposal problem. And is I may add extremely unlikely to occur. Weapons are made to be used and used they will be sooner or later so long as the formula of nationalism remains in operation and this formula can never be dissolved in terms of itself that is in political-military terms.

Italo Calvino *

In a world in which no one can be pleased with himself or at peace with his own conscience, in which no nation or institution can claim to embody a universal idea, and not even its own particular truth and nothing more, the presence of the people of Vietnam is the only one which sheds any light. There are three exemplary human images which, every day, this little country— North and South united again under the rain of bombs and of napalm—offers to our contemporaries. (1) The patient and just men of Hanoi, who by governing a country which is the victim of an exorbitant and interminable violence, show that they are the wisest, most responsible and most independent Government in existence in the world today, the only Government at the level of the situation. (2) The total guerrilla warfare of the campaigns of the South, which of all the partisan struggles of our century is the most widespread, that which has the most general support of all the inhabitants, and the most ingenious, the most inventively relentless, and the most solitary, in the midst of the great world which thinks it is at peace, a population of poor rice-growers blocks the way of the greatest military power in the world; and knows that it can never win, and its enemies know that it can never be defeated. (3) The absolute pacifists, the Buddhist monks who in order to utter the word peace more loudly than the sound of war express it with a new sign: the flames of their own bodies sprinkled with petrol.

Of the three images, the one which impresses itself on our experience as the newest—and the most violent —is that of the absolute pacifist. But its evidence reverberates also on the other two figures; it emphasizes how in them too the exemplary character is in this halo of fire which makes them alone, even though they are only a stone's throw distant from us: no one is more solitary than he who carries on guerrilla warfare while the rest of the world is not at war; and no one is more alone than the just man who remains just under the blows of injustice.

In this solitude lies the strength of Vietnam as an image of our conscience; but perhaps it is also its real strength. Perhaps the true solutions will be able to emerge from there, from what Vietnam tells us that is new and extreme. I would not be able to say more; I am only a man who reflects on images, on the only signs which he succeeds in distinguishing. I know that only one situation would be worse than this false world peace: a real world war. For everybody, and for Vietnam, a world war would burn in the general crucible the seed of this its solitary strength. But even an agreement at the summit between the "Great Powers"—the only solution that logic can suggest and hope for and impatiently await—will sanction only a new compromise of the relations of force above the ruins and the tombs, if it does not bear the imprint of Vietnamese invincibility, in its triple aspect: the serene wisdom of Ho Chi Minh, the guerrilla warfare without quarter of the Vietcong, the absolute flame of the Buddhist monk.

James Cameron

I am bitterly opposed to the war in Vietnam in all its aspects. I hold it to be atrocious, senseless, pitiful and

perilous, and certain to become more so. I say this having seen it and been in its midst, both in the South and the North divisions of the country. It is a brutal imposition of power politics on a small country, and by now it has demoralized aggressors and victims alike, and I have pity on them both.

It could be brought to an end by the application of the normal conventions of international behavior, by the implementation of the Agreements made in Geneva in 1954, which provided for the withdrawal of all foreign armies from both sides of a temporary frontier and the unification of Vietnam through free elections. This solution is unlikely to come about, since the US has committed too much investment in men and money and prestige. Vietnam therefore remains an area of darkness and pain, and the anteroom of the Third and Last Great War.

Camilo José Cela *

I do not accept any sort of intervention by anyone in the affairs of anyone else, though I do not deny the interdependence of all affairs and situations, distant as they may appear, within a given period of time. If the UN were, in fact, an organism serving peace, it would be up to it to intervene in Vietnam to restore order, or at least minimal elementary order (public order), subsequently making possible essential or inherent order (juridical, conscient order). But the UN is not a sound organism, but rather a sick one (it would, perhaps, be better to say a poorly built one), manipulated by two species of adventurers, both of them natural enemies of man: the politicians and the functionaries. Just as it is not conceivable, in accord with strict justice, to fight against police states (Hitler's Germany, Stalin's Russia) with the procedures proper to police states, neither is it conceivable to fight war with war. The opposite of war (and also its antidote) is peace, never a counterwar. Humanity, which is not, unfortunately, very mature as regards the profitable enjoyment of peace, has been deceived by the fallacy that peace can be imposed by war, forgetful of the fact that war only engenders more wars as well as hunger and destruction and, in the end, the peace of the tomb and the dominion of the police. Even if one were to admit—after not a little moral suasion—that peace could ever be achieved by means of war, it should not be forgotten that any such curious war-in-search-of-peace would first have to be depersonalized and made aseptic. This hypothesis, monstrous as well as logical, would lead us to conclude that it is not acceptable, for as long as the UN exists and while the possibility also exists of making it flexible and effective, to have anyone else arrogate to itself the role of gendarme to the world. The entire world knows that this falsely heroic and falsely self-abnegating attitude conceals a design which should be proscribed: imperialism.

The war should be resolved, either by imposing the iron and depersonalized presence of the UN (a not very likely eventuality) or by leaving the Vietnamese alone, after first effectively blockading their coasts and frontiers. Less blood would inevitably flow in a struggle between Vietnamese alone than in a battle between Vietnamese supported on one side and the other by their complex alliances. The false Solomonic solution (East Germany and West Germany, North Korea and South Korea, North Vietnam and South Vietnam) is no more than a heavy-handed makeshift in which the final solution proves ever elusive, and constitutes a situation in which the fierce raven of hatred makes a nest, whence one day, we can assume, it will again caw. The ideological partitioning of countries—never carried out in an absolute, but always in a contingent, manner —is no solution but rather a warren of troubles, a hatchery of problems which tend to seek a solution by making a clean slate of all previous assumptions, as these are repugnant to the immediate sense of reality. Nationalisms—and their sequels of heroism and ineptitude—are still too close to the very skin of our flesh to bear forgetting. For my part I understand politics as a pragmatic matter, and thus my answers: The question is, I think, how I *believe* the conflict in Vietnam should be resolved, not how I would *wish* it to be.

Paddy Chayefsky

I think we are in Vietnam to set up a large force in Southeast Asia in preparation for war with China. If there is to be such a war, we mean to confine it within conventional techniques, which in turn means before the Chinese have a sufficient nuclear establishment to cause the unimaginable consequences of a nuclear war. In the curious way of the world today, that is actually a moral position.

This policy is of course predicated on the belief the Chinese would start a nuclear war if they were capable and if it served their sense of historic purpose. (If our leaders are to be considered paranoid in this belief and consequently irresponsible, what is one to expect from the Chinese leaders who are far more paranoid and consequently far more irresponsible? I don't think

American anxieties about the possibility of a Chinese-started nuclear war are unrealistic. And I also believe it is necessary to make a clear showing of our resoluteness of spirit to the Chinese so that they will make no further mistakes about that in formulating their own future policies.)

However, the war in Vietnam seems a poor way of achieving these military and diplomatic goals. We can base a large armed force in Southeast Asia without this war, and we can be resolute of spirit without being suicidal.

In the simplest terms, I do not believe any man's son is worth sacrificing in order to achieve merely tactical advantages in the endless skirmishing between the great powers. There is nothing elemental to the American identity at stake in Vietnam.

I am therefore against our involvement in Vietnam because there is nothing there worth any American's death in battle.

John Cheever

I am against the United States intervention in Vietnam but I am not in any way well enough informed to propose a way of ending the war.

Haakon Chevalier

The United States in Vietnam is waging a ruthless aggressive war against a small, peace-loving country, in violation of all the rules and laws that should govern relations between nations. It is a war of mass extermination and wholesale destruction.

The people of Vietnam have shown exemplary courage in resisting this aggression. The only hope that I see of saving what is left of Vietnam is for the people of the world to exert such pressure of condemnation on the American Government that it will be forced to cease its aggression and negotiate with those it is fighting.

Robert Conquest

1. I fully support the Americans, and believe that all except convinced anti-democrats would do the same but for an unremitting barrage of straight falsehoods

and selected facts; partially interpreted legalisms; and atrocity propaganda; all compounded by ignorance of (or reluctance to face) the realities of totalitarian politics and war. (You yourselves are not exempt: to seek the public opinions of Soviet writers is, for obvious reasons in no way reflecting on themselves, quite meaningless.)

2. Ideal: Vietnam united by UN-supervised free elections in North and South. "Free" includes (as with us) full freedom of press and organization and similar freedom for further elections later. Minimum: abandonment (as in Korea and Berlin) of the attempt to extend Communist rule into the non-Communist area.

Robert Creeley

The intervention of the United States in Vietnam tends to perpetuate a locked "vocabulary" at a time when the public consciousness of this country is admitting a most significant change. I am against the intervention, simply that it commits the United States to a policy of public falsehood and mitigates whatever integrity might otherwise serve as a measure of public behavior. Further, I do not believe in the justice of the United States' position nor do I think it represents the viable and active elements of thought in this country.

Naïvely or not, I can only believe a resolution of the conflict can come through the admission of all concerned to its discussion, either through the agency of the United Nations or by means of a supranational committee of arbitration. Coercion, misrepresentation, and private interests argue an intolerable situation, and each I feel to be active in this instance.

Robert Crichton

I don't believe the first question is any longer meaningful. There arrives a time when events move beyond conjecture and become irreversible facts. The presence of the US in Vietnam has become such a fact.

How the conflict can be ended I'm not prepared to say. Immoral or not, the solution has gone beyond a question of morality into a political and military area that at times seems beyond the control of the Governments involved.

What is not beyond the control of the American people, however, is the way this war is being conducted in their name; the manner in which people are dying.

While one is mindful of the conduct of the Germans and that of the French in Algeria, because of the nature of the weapons now being used on the people of South and lately North, Vietnam, the war in Vietnam has now become in many respects the most immoral ever waged by one people on another. Sartre has defined evil as the systematic substitution of the abstract for the concrete and it is this we are allowing the military to do in Vietnam. The instruments we are using on the people go beyond mutilating their bodies; they probe to the heart of what we term Western civilization. Any society capable of using such weapons and devices, and becoming *committed* to them, must eventually succumb to the sickness of its own violence. France found this out in Algeria. Something has gone out of France.

A catalogue of the arsenal of weapons now being used on the people of Vietnam will make it plain why I feel that at this stage the conduct of the war has become more important to our civilization than the fact of the war itself.

Napalm, or jellied gasoline, is the most familiar of the antipersonnel weapons. Napalm is "delivered" on villages in aluminum tanks triggered by white phosphorus bombs. On impact the bomb explodes and the now flaming jellied gasoline consumes everything it comes in contact with. The effect on flesh is similar to that of a blowtorch or flamethrower but more tenacious. Nothing is wasted. Fragments of the phosphorus bomb itself, if they penetrate the body, will not stop burning for days, even after death, even in the grave. Military terminology makes it hard for people to visualize the effects of these raids but the terminology at air bases is more vivid. Villages are bathed in napalm; "Charlie" is barbecued.

While napalm is the most famous, the little-understood CBU's are the most effective weapon and the favorite of the fliers. CBU means "cluster bomb unit" and each CBU is a canister filled with some 800 metal balls, each the size of a grapefruit. Inside each grapefruit is a cluster of smaller metal balls called bombets. When the jet approaches the village, the canister is opened, the 800 balls are dropped on the houses with the speed of the jet and at low altitude are exploded by compressed air, showering the village with the smaller steel balls. A CBU is designed to kill or maim any living thing, indoors or out, on an extended path several hundred feet wide. In some CBU's little steel needles are used instead of bombets. Spinning at a speed of 1,000 m.p.h., a single needle can sever the hand of a child, and there are millions of them. When they are used properly, an entire area can be "lawnmowered" with CBU's.

Were these used only on fortified troops, they could

perhaps be justified, but they are used on villages in suspect areas because of a tactic called "reconnaissance by fire"—which means just what it says: shoot and ask questions later. If, after a CBU is dropped, people run, the pilot is allowed to assume he has officially flushed Vietcong and the village may be strafed, bathed with napalm and mopped up with 20-mm. cannon shells which can be fired into the homes of the people at a rate of 4,000 to 6,000 rounds a minute.

Perhaps the least understood weapon is the use of the B-52. Designed as a strategic weapon to carry high-explosive bombs to such targets as bridges and rail centers, it is being used in South Vietnam instead to obliterate "unsympathetic" areas. Since each plane is capable of dropping 60,000 pounds of incendiaries, once called "fire bombs," fire storms have been created in areas as huge as 30 square miles, storms in which the heat has risen to thousands of degrees and storms from which it is conceded that nothing human or animal or vegetable can survive. The number of women and children who have been burned to death this way will never be known. So terrible is the damage that nothing is left, the balance of nature will never return, and these parts of their world are lost to them forever.

I find it hard to believe the President knows the manner in which these weapons are being used on the people of Vietnam. But this must be naïve. The decision of mid-February to "step up" the bombing—after the failure of strategic bombing to halt infiltration was apparent—can only mean a change in manner. The first effort was to break the line of communications but the new effort will be one to break the will of the people by burning and bleeding them to death. The effort will be around the clock because when the target becomes people, darkness doesn't matter. Perhaps it will work; enough blood will flow and burning be done to break the spirit of the people. And perhaps just as likely, for a nation with the burden of a Hiroshima and Nagasaki already to bear, this burning might become unbearable, and something will go out of America that will never return.

Rupert Croft-Cooke

1. Entirely and wholeheartedly *for,* though I could do without the high-sounding and much publicized motives for intervention, to "contain communism in Southeast Asia," to "free the people of South Vietnam from the Communist yoke," and so on. The issue is an entirely realistic one—a mob of marauding gangsters who try to appropriate the wealth of their neighbors must be suppressed and the United States alone has the power and the will to do the job. Civilian suffering is inevitable but would be infinitely greater if the evil had been allowed to grow. Had some power had the foresight and courage to do in Europe in 1936 what the US is doing in Vietnam now, incalculable human suffering would have been saved. It is not a matter of taking sides. For all I know, the South Vietnamese Government may be corrupt and unrepresentative. But the South Vietnamese did not invade or threaten invasion. They did not use propaganda to attract their young men into a phony idealism in order to wage war for the ancient and disgraceful motives of power and gain.

2. By force of arms, as quickly and humanely as possible. However reactionary and unimaginative this may appear, it is the only policy that can bring peace to Vietnam, or bring the Peace of the World nearer.

David Daiches

I am against the military activities of the United States in Vietnam. The issue is a complicated one and I cannot believe that any facile black-and-white picture is remotely adequate. From all accounts, the present Government of Air Vice-Marshal Ky is harsh and unrepresentative and the Air Vice-Marshal himself is not a man who can be respected by anyone of liberal opinions. The conflict in Vietnam seems to be a civil conflict, and there seems little doubt that there is great cruelty practiced on either side. The Americans themselves have admitted the appalling human suffering caused by their own bombing of "suspected" villages —suffering caused to South Vietnam civilians whom the American forces are supposed to be saving. This is a dirty and cruel war, which neither side can win and which, in addition to causing frightful suffering, prevents an otherwise obtainable slackening of the Cold War between America and the USSR and steadily increases the danger of a third world war.

The immediate step I should like to see taken is the unconditional stopping of American bombing. The aim as I see it should be the neutralization of a unified Vietnam.

Len Deighton

The US intervention in Vietnam was neither benign nor clever. The present situation is morally wrong as well as exceedingly dangerous, but it would be a mistake to imagine that there is now any lasting solution that would be quick or easy, or one that can be described in a few words.

There are men of bad will on both sides who wish the war to continue and public statements by individuals or groups are often cynically utilized by such men. Antiwar sentiments of an oversimplified, ingenuous type can have the reverse effect of the one intended.

Babette Deutsch

I am emphatically against the intervention of the United States in Vietnam.

Although I know that the situation there is too complicated to enable a layman to say how the conflict should be resolved, I am convinced that the first step to take is to stop bombing. This should be done at once. Further, I believe that we should promptly scale down the fighting, and should work intensively for an early discussion of the issues by all the parties concerned, including the Vietcong and the Buddhists. The war in Vietnam is a civil war, exacerbated by our intervention, and must be treated as such, the chief efforts being directed toward the establishment of peace.

Isaac Deutscher

I am, of course, against the intervention of the United States in Vietnam. That intervention is the most barbarous act of warfare since the Second World War; the most shameless denial by the world's greatest power of the right of a small nation to independence and self-determination; and an act of the most intense class struggle waged by America's capitalist-monopolistic oligarchy (and its servants and puppets) against Vietnam's peasants and toilers—a war between palaces and huts. American imperialism has no right to occupy even an inch of Vietnamese soil.

The conflict in Vietnam can be resolved only by a total American withdrawal. This would leave the Vietnamese people to make their own decision about their own destiny and to make their own choice between revolution and counterrevolution. I have no doubt that left to themselves the Vietnamese will choose revolution, as they have repeatedly chosen it in the past.

Peter De Vries

The pedigree of errors is a long one. A decade ago we opposed the election prescribed by the Geneva Conference on the ground that it would result in a Communistic government, but it is interesting, in the light of recent events, to speculate on what that might in turn have led to. Given the strong nationalistic thrust of Vietnamese revolutionaries and the instinctive fear of being sucked into the Peking vacuum cleaner, a fresh young Marxist regime not dependent on China for support against a Western power might by now be contributing its bit toward the decentralization of world communism, along with North Korea, Yugoslavia, and, of course, China herself. The suspicion even begins to form in one's mind that the way to contain Red China might be with a ring of left-wing states. We for our part, at any rate, are doing our best to unify that squabbling family. With every bomb we drop in a war that apparently can never be won, we are driving Hanoi closer to Peking, and more Vietnamese nationalists into the National Liberation Front. Given time, we might even heal the breach between Peking and Moscow.

I think we should stop all bombing instantly (the lunacy of supposing it could destroy the will to fight should be clear to anyone able to imagine what bombs raining on American soil would do to ours) and limit any military activities to a defensive perimeter behind which to escalate the war against poverty and against social and political misery and inequality in that tormented land. This means rallying the basic nationalistic aspirations of the Vietnamese people behind somebody other than an avowed admirer of Hitler—that man shoulder-to-shoulder with whom the hawks fancy themselves as resisting a new Munich.

Daphne du Maurier

Although I am in principle *against* the intervention of the United States or any *other* power in the war in Vietnam, I do not feel I am sufficiently well-informed on the subject to make a statement.

Nell Dunn

I am horrified by all the fighting and frightened by all wars and therefore instead of confronting the reality —I close my ears and eyes and live wrongly in my private world.

Richard Eberhart

I am against the war in Vietnam and think we should take the initiative in withdrawing step by step. I think we became the aggressors when we bombed North Vietnam. In World War II, I had a passionate belief in the evils of Hitlerism. There was no doubt in my mind. I volunteered and served four years in the Naval Reserve as an aerial free-gunnery training officer.

We will have to get over the notion of wars in the future just as we will have to get over the idea of nationalism. There have been just wars and unjust wars and I do not believe that man is not a combative angel. World War II was a just war as Nazi ideas were so evil that they had to be overcome. In the Vietnam situation there is doubt in my mind as there is doubt in the minds of many. I have never been a political poet but now politics is forced upon us.

If you looked at the map of the world in World War II you could see who would win. If you look at the map of the world now you may wonder what we are doing in Asia. Americans do not yet realize that the great majority of the peoples of the world are not white. We do not yet realize that American power could be put to better uses than to kill even one Vietnamese.

In August I was unexpectedly invited by the Peace Corps to East Africa to view our volunteers in Kenya. Based on Nairobi and flying in small planes or going over rugged terrain by Land Rover I visited many volunteers and had the greatest respect for these intelligent young men serving other people disinterestedly on land-settlement schemes and in schools under the principle of giving not getting, with a desire to help because of love, not to kill for any reason. I am for the Peace Corps, not for the present war.

Richard Ellmann

The intentions of the United States in Vietnam were originally benign, but they have been warped by the bellicosity of incompetent South Vietnamese leaders, and by the momentum of a military effort which has little popular support in Vietnam and not much here in the United States. The war is as impossible to win in military terms as to defend in moral ones. While withdrawal is not easy, I think we must withdraw, to save not only thousands of lives but also our sense of reality and of national conscience. We should immediately stop the bombing and sue for peace.

William Empson

So far as I can make out, the Americans have no right at all to spread destruction in Vietnam; a US airman who has wrecked a village with napalm there is just as much a war criminal as the accused at Nuremberg.

It is harder to answer your second question: How should the conflict be resolved? But reasonable proposals have been made, and are still being made. The essential first step is just for the Americans to stop doing evil.

Jules Feiffer

I'm against. Isn't everybody?

The solution to the problem is so simple that I'm amazed it hasn't occurred to anyone else.

Lyndon Johnson should go on nationwide TV and say to the American people, "Ah have goofed," thus ending the only real aggression in Vietnam: our own.

If he brings to his withdrawl speech the same tears and regret he brings to his escalation speeches, the American people might very well unite behind him and he probably will not be impeached.

Lawrence Ferlinghetti

Meanwhile back at the Ranch the then President also known as Colonel Cornpone got out a blank Army draft and began to fill in the spaces with men and Colonel Cornpone got down to the bottom of the order where there is a space to indicate just where the troops are to be sent and Colonel Cornpone got a faraway look in his eye and reached out and started spinning a globe of the world and his eye wandered over the spinning surface of the world and after a long time he said I See No Relief so they brought him a relief map of the world and he looked at it a long time and said Thank You Gentlemen I see it all very clearly now yes indeed everything stands out very clearly now and I can see the oceans themselves rolling back and Western Civilization still marching Westward around the world and the New Frontier now truly knows no boundaries and those there Vietnamese don't stand a Chinaman's chance in Hell but still there's all these Chinamen who think they do and also think they can actually reverse the Westward march of civilization and actually reverse the natural Westward spin of our globe but Gentlemen these are not War Games this is not Space Angels this is the real thing Gentlemen and I know right exactly where this here Vietnam is Gentlemen and I want to make doubly sure that all our own people know right exactly where this here Vietnam is Gentlemen in case any of you should happen to get cornered by some eggheads or someone And just then Ladybird came running and Colonel Cornpone stepped into the cloakroom and whispered to her The world really does rotate Westward don't it? and she being smarter than he as is usually the case whispered back that this here Vietnam was not a place but a state of mind and Colonel Cornpone got that old faraway look again and stepped back onto the front porch and sat there rocking for a long time and then said Gentlemen I am a family man and this is for real and I am hereby ordering the complete and final liberation of Vietmind I mean Vietnam for the roots of the trouble are found wherever the landless and oppressed the poor and despised stand before the gates of opportunity and are not allowed across the Frontier into the Great Society which seems to lie out before me like a land of dreams and so Gentlemen here we go fasten your seat belts we are powerful and free and united there ain't much we can't do and so Gentlemen let me point out to you exactly where it is we all are going on this here globe because Gentlemen even though I am reputed never to have been out of the United States I do know right where we are going on the brink of Vietmind I mean Vietnam and even though we don't want to stop the world spinning in the right direction even for an instant I do want to slow it down just long enough for me to put my finger for you right on this here sore spot which is Vietmine I mean Vietnam and Colonel Cornpone put out his hand to slow down the world just a bit but this world would not be slowed down a bit this world would not stop spinning at all and Texas and Vietnam spun on together faster and faster slipping away under Colonel Cornpone's hand because the surface of this world had suddenly become very very slippery with a strange kind of red liquid that ran on it across all the obscene boundaries and this world went on spinning faster and faster in the same so predestined direction and kept on spinning and spinning and spinning and spinning!

Leslie A. Fiedler

It is important first to know that the people of Vietnam can effectively choose only between two forms of political indignity, two modes of terror. It is irrelevant

morally and even in the long run strategically that the administrators of one form of terror are "friendly" to the United States—i.e., will take our money—just as it is irrelevant that the administrators of the other form of terror speak of themselves as Communists or are comparatively less effective or have darker skins than some of us others.

What is to be done? *Get out.*

Gabriel Fielding

I am against the intervention of the United States in Vietnam. Although as a Catholic I am against the philosophy of Marxism I believe that unrestricted capitalism is a luxury which evolving societies can no longer afford and that conversely communism, with all its defects, is part of the political and social evolution of mankind. I believe therefore that US intervention in the Far East is disingenuous and tragic both for the United States itself and for the Vietnamese.

In my opinion the conflict in Vietnam should be resolved round the conference table. Since ultimately it is the rich man who must accommodate and disarm the poor, I believe that at the conference table it should be the United States' role to continue to promise economic aid to the peoples of Vietnam whether under a no doubt temporary Communist regime or under some compromise "democratic" Government. Only in this way can the United States prove that it has the interests of men and women at heart and thus finally prove the superiority of its philosophy and intentions to the peasant political demagogues of the Far East.

Constantine FitzGibbon

The question about American intervention in Vietnam is so baldly and loosely put as to make any sensible answer impossible. Naturally it is deplorable that American soldiers and airmen should be killing and dying in Southeast Asia. On the other hand it may well be that this tragedy has averted, is averting or will avert an even more appalling tragedy on a much more massive scale. I am not in a position to know whether this is so or not. No more are the other writers to whom this naïve question has been addressed. I do know that the American Government consists, on the whole, of men of good will, while the Communist Governments consist of evil men. I know also that the Communists and their sympathizers here object to

American intervention in Vietnam. It therefore follows that this intervention damages the Communists' cause, for they never object on humanitarian grounds, and so on that basis one may assume that there is some marginal advantage in what is nevertheless essentially a tragic predicament.

The conflict in Vietnam can be resolved only when the Communist powers in the northern part of that state, in the other Indochinese states, and in Red China decide that the continued use of violence to achieve their aims in South Vietnam is no longer profitable to them. Once they shall have reached this elementary conclusion, and have proved that they intend to alter their policy, presumably the Americans could, should and will withdraw their forces from that unhappy land. Certainly that is the solution which the majority of Americans and, I imagine, of South Vietnamese would most like to see.

John Fowles

Well-phrased declarations of outrage are too easy to write; and once written, make it too easy to forget the cause of outrage. At this stage asking people whether they are for or against American intervention is in any case as irrelevant as asking whether they are for or against the solar system. We are in the solar system; and not able to *do* anything by declaring ourselves for or against it.

The only practical solution is the establishment of a permanent United Nations standing army. The world is now melted small, one overcrowded city; and no civilized city can exist without a police force. Obviously the politicians and diplomats, from Washington to Peking, will fight tooth and nail to stop us ever having a force capable of neutralizing violence. They want power, not peace. Wolves never brought bread to the shepherd's door.

Pamela Frankau

I am against the war in Vietnam because I am against all wars, no matter how, where or why they are fought.

As to an opinion on the resolving of the present conflict, I have none; being a skeptic toward all save God; who would not appear to have been consulted in this matter.

Northrop Frye

I am strongly against the war in Vietnam, which is being waged with a brutality justified only by a "they do it too" type of argument, and which makes America's role in the Nuremberg trials twenty years ago the most miserable hypocrisy. It is a genocidal war, one which the Americans cannot win, and which they keep on fighting only because of some obsession about face-saving. Its public support is simply the result of the bloodshed itself, i.e., it is very difficult to accept the fact that one's fellow countrymen are dying for nothing.

I think the conflict should be resolved by a planned series of strategic withdrawals with the final objective of getting out of Southeast Asia and reverting to the Monroe Doctrine. The reason for gradual withdrawal would be to try to build up some of the social infrastructures that would enable Vietnam to survive as a democracy. The notion that Vietnam would inevitably go Communist if there were any withdrawal at all is not necessarily true: the examples of Malaysia and Indonesia indicate that social movements are more complicated in that part of the world than public opinion thinks. In any case, the continued presence of an American army in South Vietnam is a continuous source of demoralization, and the propping up of a corrupt and unpopular regime, as the example of Chiang Kai-shek ought to have shown long ago, will only make a Communist takeover eventually inevitable, far more bloody when it occurs, and much more aggressive and imperialistic in its mood when it does come.

David Garnett

I am strongly against the continued intervention by the United States in Vietnam. The evils of the war are not confined to Asia and to the expenditure of American lives and treasure, but are most damaging to the United States itself. The war results in the United States appearing to many peoples as a ruthless militaristic power and disguises the real nature of American concern for the welfare of humanity. It divides the educated people of the United States and destroys their influence and their power for good.

The war should be ended by negotiation among the people of Vietnam itself and by the withdrawal of the United States armed forces.

Allen Ginsberg

1. US intervention in Vietnam was always a mistake because the motives were wrong from the very beginning and the consequences of our actions have compounded the original miscalculation to such a tangle that no one in his right mind or wrong mind could follow all the threads anymore. Bad Karma, bad Karma for the States.

The original mistake was the Dulles-Eisenhower apocalyptic barroom brawl hysteria psychology aided and abetted by three catholics namely Max Lerner Cardinal Spellman and Henry Luce and one negro the head of Freedom House Leo Cherne. Now they all got together in the mid-fifties and broadcast to everybody some very complicated series of doctrines which wound up in my poor father's mind—he reads Television—that in order to "contain" China—see, everybody wanted to "contain" China—we had to surround China with christian capitalist Western-oriented Governments such as the Diem government which the above-mentioned Jewish gentlemen promoted. By the time all this thinking got formulated consciously so that it arrived in my brainpan it came in the form of this sort of language: that in the struggle between China & American Freedom Power, Neutralism was unacceptable. Only those guys on OUR side were acceptable, to form governments surrounding China, to contain China. Active people, who were really *against* China and with us. Now, we really insisted on that, we spent money, sent spies, armies, etc. It was announced officially in *Life* magazine; everybody read it at the Dentist. *Time* magazine had big discussions about neutralism unacceptable. Everybody insulted India for a year. Everybody had to be with us or against us.

Naturally such a humorless foreign policy, smacking of outright paranoia if not, at the least, total lack of self-control, could lead to nothing but more and more reality-complications, an escalation of aggressive hysteria to jabberwockian heights limited only by the physical nature of the universe.

What's really disgusting is the tone of perplexed sincerity adopted by *Time* & *Life* senior editors A.D. 1966 to explain that we're in it too deep to pull out now even if we shouldn't be in it. Meanwhile the Peking Universe is also swept by winds of paranoia emanating from Henry Luce's brain. Mao Tse-tung and Henry Luce both think the root of the struggle is a geopolitical mystical struggle between the emanations of the yellow virus life form and the white virus life form, and that it makes a difference if their own side wins.

US intervention in Vietnam was always a mistake because the motives were wrong from the very beginning and the consequences etc.

2. The way to end the war has less to do with the situation in Vietnam than it has to do with the situation of internal propaganda, attitudinizing, brainwash, image-manipulation, news control etc. within the United States. How the entire communications & media apparatus have been able to sustain a sympathetic Myth rationalization for our part in the two-way paranoia for over a decade, is a little mysterious. It took a lot of doubletalk, from the mid-50's on, to make the whole dream of Vietnam seem like normal everyday waking consciousness. It would be necessary to bomb out the entire public consciousness of the USA with LSD or some therapeutic equivalent like Burroughs' Cut-up method before we could expect the beginning of self-examination on the part of the majority of our populace who are, after all, enjoying some artificial prosperity as by-product of hostility to China.

I mean we don't want to share what we got so we'll overeat a little.

Elections in South Vietnam, as reported in the NY *Times,* excluded all candidates who proposed reconciliation with Vietcong or Neutralism. One step toward resolving the armed conflict would be to promote elections which would lead to a government which would want to end the conflict.

We could even do what the Buddhists proposed, stay in Vietnam to help a neutralist government sympathetic to Vietcong, or even pro-Vietcong government, reconstruct the country.

If we still are concerned with containing China, we might let Ho Chi Minh do that for us, instead of driving him into dependence on China. After all we're not fighting "Communism"—we made peace with that in Europe—we're really fighting the Yellow Life Form Virus, specifically the Chinese one.

If we're worried about betraying all our "friends" and allies in Saigon, I would be in favor of inviting them—millions if necessary—to share these States with us. A larger dash of oriental style has always been desirable here.

All in all the problem is not how to manipulate the situation in Vietnam—common sense would show a way; ways have been shown & rejected for decades. De Gaulle & The Pope could show the way if we asked them. The problem is here in America, how do we get out of ourselves, our own minds. "A new world is only a new mind."—W. C. Williams.

Paul Goodman

I am against the intervention. We should pull out. Give a haven in the US for those South Vietnamese we have rendered odious. Pay a large indemnity for some of the damage we have done—25 billion, cost of one year of the war? Then proceed to give aid in Southeast Asia according to their pace and need, to help them develop in their own way.

Robert Graves

1. I cannot venture on an opinion, since not all the relevant facts are known, either to the Government of the United States or to that of North Vietnam, much less to myself. Nor will they be known for another fifty years—if then.

Moreover the heroism and high morale of the real fighters on both sides—high-altitude bombers are not here included—suggests that neither of the armies engaged disapproves of war as such, and that few of the unmaimed survivors will regret their part in this war. As I myself have never regretted my part in World War I, though for the French and English and Russians it went on two years beyond the point where it should have been broken off; and I was severely wounded, myself.

It certainly *looks* as if the same point has been reached in the present war; and its continuance seems to invite Chinese intervention as ours once invited American intervention. The Vietnamese struggle against enormous odds has encouraged Chinese militarism, a phenomenon of Western origin and contrary to age-old Chinese tradition, like Chinese communism. Nevertheless—

2. Nothing but time can resolve the conflict, since national honor is at stake on both sides. And to ask the opinion of writers, however well-informed, seems unreasonable. As it was when *Authors Take Sides on the Spanish War* was published in 1937. Who could have foreseen that Franco's victory in the Civil War, deplored by most English and French writers, would result in his denying Hitler control of the Mediterranean and thus assuring an Allied victory?

Graham Greene

I am completely against the intervention of the United States in Vietnam. I see no excuse whatever for the presence of foreign troops on the soil of this country.

The excuse of containing communism assumes that communism is everywhere an evil. Anyone with experience of Vietnam knows this is not the case. Anyway most of us would prefer rule by our countrymen, even though Communist, than by a foreign power.

The conflict in Vietnam can only be resolved by the complete and unconditional withdrawal of American troops. If Britain had intervened in the American Civil War on the side of the South—at one time it seemed possible—would Abraham Lincoln have agreed to negotiate the future of his country with a *British* government? Hanoi is just as close in blood to Saigon as New York to Richmond. The presence of foreign troops prevents negotiations between North and South.

Geoffrey Grigson

Wars, or massacres, or murders, or bitter divisions have been caused in the past by whether cows should be sacrosanct, whether *filioque* should be added to the Creed, and whether foreskins should be clipped. Also by making short words into jet engines of the most lethal emotion; which appears, fore and aft, to have caused the situation in Vietnam. I do not myself believe the collective protestations of the American Government, which is tipsy with white words to describe its own exclusive virtue, and red words to describe the exclusive evil of other societies—so tipsy that Americans extend the violence of their own backward society into this filthy Vietnamese war. One may also disbelieve Moscow and Peking. But America claims to be more grown-up, more civilized, and should go off the bottle. If you start, you can stop. There is no war when you stop. (I write also as one whose six brothers have been killed by the extension of political foolishness and word-mouthing and hypocrisy into such organized murder.)

Stuart Hampshire

I am opposed to the intervention of the United States in Vietnam, because, firstly, the probability that this intervention would lead to a democratic and progressive regime in South Vietnam has always been much too low to justify the horrifying destruction and misery involved; secondly, because the war prolongs the Cold War and increases the risks of atomic war; thirdly, because this undeclared war sets an example of illegality and of defiance of the United Nations; fourthly, because of the corrupting effect of the lies that are officially promulgated, and because of the vast waste of resources which would otherwise have been used for social progress in the United States, and elsewhere. It seems to me a stupid war, prolonged by the folly of believing what generals and admirals say.

The conflict should be resolved by the United States abandoning its attempt to win the war, holding a defensive position, guaranteeing the protection of its local allies and making known, secretly or openly, its readiness to negotiate with the Vietcong or NLF on condition that they accept UN or neutral supervision of the safety and fair treatment of the United States' local allies.

Roy Harrod

1. I am strongly in favor of the US intervention in Vietnam.

2. The conflict in Vietnam should be resolved by American victory.

On my estimates of what I have heard, I base the following opinions:

1. The war that the Americans are fighting in Vietnam is the most worthwhile war that has been fought in this century, apart from that against Hitler;
2. The vast mass of Vietnamese *long* for the Americans to win;
3. The Vietnamese are in the pathetic position of having no governmental machinery of their own: they depend *entirely* on what the Americans do for them. (How far the French are to blame for having left Indochina thus defenseless I cannot judge);
4. If the Americans let us down (by "us" I mean right-thinking people) it would not only involve the millions of Vietnamese themselves in nameless suffering, but it would also give a ghastly tribute to the effectiveness of dictatorships in using all the beastly techniques of subversion, infiltration and fifth column for overpowering a people that wants to be free;
5. I don't think that the conflict will or can be resolved at all quickly. One must argue against those who desire an "escalation" to bring it to an end quickly. It may have to go on for a dozen years or so, during which time the Americans can teach the Vietnamese to desire their own machinery of government. This is a slow process;
6. Finally, in relation to a long conflict, may I protest strongly against sob stuff about civilian casualties. The Vietnamese are a brave and

pugnacious people. If it could be put to the vote, which it can't be, I am sure that they would opt for a thousand times as many civilian casualties as have yet occurred (and I include North Vietnam in this) in a *good cause*.

Joseph Heller

1. I am *against* the military intervention of the US in Vietnam. It was a ghastly choice, and thousands die each month because of it.

2. By getting US soldiers out: reduce offensive military operations to create a stalemate, turn the problem over to the other countries, whose officials are better able than our own to act intelligently in this situation, and get out *fast*.

We ought to stop murdering Asians. We ought to stop sending young American boys, against their will, ten thousand miles away to be killed and mutilated in battle against people that do not threaten us and did us no harm. We ought to stop squandering billions of dollars every month for no better purpose than to dignify cruel follies and miscalculations. By fighting and attempting to justify this war of ours in Vietnam, we are reducing ourselves to the low moral level of Nazis.

It was Lyndon Johnson's bad fortune to take us into this dreadful national catastrophe; if only he has the good taste to bring us back out!

Nat Hentoff

1. I am against the intervention of the United States in Vietnam, as I was against the intervention of the United States in Cuba and the Dominican Republic. Neither by international law nor by the Charter of the United Nations is such intervention in any way justified. I am also convinced that under the Charter and Judgment of the Nuremberg Trials, any American who takes part in the killing and other destruction that is a corollary of our intervention is guilty of international crimes. I am convinced, furthermore, that no amount of underlining the killing and destruction caused by the other side justifies this country's involvement, for it is this country's involvement which has so horrifyingly accelerated the amount of killing and destruction on all sides.

The argument that we are defending a "free" Government of South Vietnam is absurd in the face of the overwhelming weight of information to the contrary from non-Communist reporters over many years. We are, on the other hand, intervening without right—except right of force which is no right—in what is essentially a civil war.

2. The American Government must take the first unilateral step to move toward the resolution of the conflict. That step is a total, permanent stop to the bombing of both North Vietnam and "enemy" territory in South Vietnam.

From that point on, the most intelligent suggestion I've seen, in the context of present reality, is David Schoenbrun's in the Fall 1966 issue of *The Columbia University Forum*. He advocates that there be "the beginnings of a negotiation among the Vietnamese themselves by themselves, between the NLF and Saigon in the South and also between South and North. . . . The only way such negotiations could succeed . . . would be to quarantine Vietnam off from the world power competition, that is to neutralize it." Thereby "all foreign forces can be withdrawn, and Vietnam first, neighboring countries later, brought under a general great-power agreement to guarantee the neutralization of Southeast Asia."

What of China? As of this writing, it is impossible to predict what Chinese policy is going to be in view of the internal fissures there. But if the United States, simultaneously with the first steps toward the neutralization of Southeast Asia, were to abandon its attempts to keep Communist China out of the United Nations, a beginning could be made in dealing with that country's far from unjustified paranoia.

Admittedly I have not given a detailed plan for the resolution of the conflict. I doubt if a detailed plan is possible at this point. What matters most fundamentally now is that there be an end to the killing. The end of United States intervention will not end all killing in Vietnam, but it will end that amount of killing for which this country—and all its citizens—are responsible.

And what if, plans for neutralization notwithstanding, all of Vietnam were to become Communist? And what if, despite the history and protestations of North Vietnamese leaders, this Communist state were to become part of the Communist Chinese bloc? We have already seen in many diverse ways—Russia, Yugoslavia, Hungary and now inside China itself—that absolutely totalitarian Communist rule cannot endure indefinitely. And furthermore, that totalitarian Communist rule becomes less and less rigid the more a country under such rule is given time to learn from and explore its own changing experiences without having to be obsessively, defensively concerned with focusing all its resources and energies on a Cold or Hot War conflict.

The primary irony within the horror of Vietnam is

that the United States, by its intervention and subsequent escalation of that intervention, has greatly strengthened the forces and ideologies most inimical to peace throughout the world. There are more similarities than differences between Lin Piao and Lyndon Johnson.

Thor Heyerdahl

In a civilized community no man, however big, strong, or noble-minded, has the right to enter another man's house and punish him, even if the other man were a burglar or assassin. In a civilized world no nation, however big, strong, or noble-minded, should have the right to enter another nation's territory to inflict punishment by land or air, even if the other nation were a danger to its neighbor. The United Nations was created to be to the world what judge and police are to the individuals within a nation. Even the biggest, strongest, and most noble-minded should listen to the supreme judge and go by way of the police if he wants to arrest a burglar.

To my mind the conflict in Vietnam can be resolved only by both parties ending hostilities simultaneously while United Nations forces are invited to supervise peace and free elections in both North and South Vietnam.

Christopher Hill

I am against the intervention of the United States in Vietnam. Even if US claims as to their motives could be taken at their face value, it is absurd to suppose that democracy can be imposed from outside. There seems no doubt that most of the inhabitants of Vietnam would rather be red than dead. With what I take to be the true motives for US intervention—extension of the US sphere of influence, strategic containment of communism—I do not sympathize. I agree with what Harold Wilson said (in 1954, alas): "We must not join or in any way encourage an anti-Communist crusade in Asia under the leadership of the Americans or anyone else." In any case present US methods are unlikely to achieve their aims without grave danger of world war.

Ideally I should like to see the US forces driven out or completely withdrawn. Assuming this is unlikely to happen quickly enough to remove the danger of world war, I should like to see a settlement in Vietnam on the lines of the decisions of the 1954 Geneva Convention, and a neutralized Vietnam set up under international guarantee. This will presumably be possible only when China takes her place in the United Nations.

David Holbrook

For or against. Against! I have recently been in America and the jingoism there appalled and terrified me. It manifested a naïve, fatal ignorance of present-day realities only possible 3,000 miles from Europe. In no European country could you parade "The Mothers of World War II" in a lorry: and nowhere else could newspaper leaders appear of the kind you read in the *Chicago Tribune* on "The American Mettle."

The great industrial and financial powers in America, urging their politicians from the background, play on this naïve jingoism, in promoting their wars here and there intended to "contain communism." For them the wars help to test strength, equipment and tactics; to draw attention away from the consequences of corruption, neglect and bad government at home; to consolidate the nation, so that it feels it has a common identity (even pleasant and otherwise humane people say savage things against "Communists" in America). War maintains a false boost to a rickety economy as is so often recognized in financial comment there. The wars also provide a symbolic externalization of the fear and hate which lurk beneath the cosmetic surface of American life. They go with that divided conscience by which America lives—the neat opulence of suburbia only being possible because of the wastes of slums and poverty at home, and the wastes of corruption and destruction caused by American arrogance abroad.

Before I went to America I felt there must be an energy of democratic sincerity and integrity of principle there, in which there was hope. I came home dismayed, for it seemed to me that there was simply insufficient discrimination there to prevent America pouring out hate and evil into the world—even to the extent of being prepared to sacrifice the world's very survival, to preserve the American way of maintaining a sense of identity—which is mostly achieved at the expense of others.

Social responsibility, humane care and service, a disinterested concern for culture, learning and education—these count for little in America, where good government is distrusted, and graft prevents even such urgently needed developments as housing schemes. Despite its claims, in its relationships with the world America is not motivated by an essential concern for human rights and equality, in terms of the needs and potentialities of beings and life, but by power. So, they will buy out nations where they can, corrupt where

they can, burn and torture where they can, and poison or deliberately spread disease where they can. They are utterly not to be trusted, and are unlikely to be restrained from destroying the world unless a majority of large nations can, by material and forceful sanctions, force them to behave, internationally.

One tries to hope for a change to come from within America; but here the most disturbing feature is that contempt for opinion, ideas and thought at large manifested by a society in which pragmatic utilitarianism and *laissez-faire* are triumphant. Education in America has been badly neglected and startlingly lacks those traditions and kinds of content which foster inquiring and challenging minds: The craven intellectual sellout at the time of McCarthy was symptomatic.

How should the conflict be resolved? Britain could take a leading part here, if our leadership were not so nervously concerned not to offend the American Government and risk disturbing the holy precinct of American financial investment in England. Of course, for a substantial body of nations to meet together to reject and condemn America would cause a world economic crisis, as America tried (as she tries now with France) to corrupt, wreck, or undermine them—as a penalty for not fawning to Uncle Sam and bowing to American policies.

But Britain could have led such a group of nations; and what a relief it would be to grapple with such a consequent crisis! What a clean feeling one would have in Europe if a group of nations coldly dissociated themselves from Uncle Sam in his Far Eastern antics! But nothing so clear comes from the Labour Government, who have chosen to forfeit the world's future in consequence. I was deeply shocked to read, when in Rome in 1965, of Harold Wilson's endorsement of American policy in Vietnam. What dismay and contempt one found around one, at England's sycophancy!

Mr. Brown's new points * are concerned more to preserve Mr. Brown and to keep the Labour Party in power than to meet the situation—for who is going to negotiate under a threat of the resumption of bombing if negotiation fails?

America, believing so much in "mettle" and gallantry, is not going to withdraw. Every proposal from the West is based on the assumption that Hanoi will be

* The British Foreign Secretary's proposals, first forward at the Labour Party Conference at Brighton on October 6, 1966, and repeated before the United Nations General Assembly on October 11, consisted of three main points: A conference between all the interested parties, a cessation of the bombing of the North, and an end to the introduction of US and North Vietnamese troops into South Vietnam. —Eds.

broken. The proposals sound like armistice proposals, with a tinge of conditional surrender about them. Just as they wasted thousands of lives on Omaha Beach in Normandy because they refused to have waterproofed engineer tanks, the Americans will sacrifice thousands of lives in Vietnam rather than lose face, or risk any suspicion of hesitation that might be interpreted as "cowardice." To them peace doesn't yet seem tolerable. War is an expression of the American *raison d'être*—because American society lacks a peaceful sense of identity so badly. So, the more American "boys" are killed, the more jingoistic the local feeling in their newspapers, the more excitement in *Life,* the more impossible it will be to withdraw—or to act sanely in diplomacy. Few Americans know what it is like to be bombed, blown up, invaded or to have one's country wasted. Mentally they are back in the "Spirit of '76": a fatal anachronism. No wonder they are so preoccupied with the dinosaur: *tyrannus rex* could be their symbol.

Only the most forcible group of nations, called together by such a power as Britain or France, could so alarm the Americans by the threat of sanctions and material resistance (I mean economic resistance—which is where it will hurt them), could force the Americans to look at the Vietnam situation realistically. And here "realistic" means that they must stop bombing and withdraw the preponderance of their forces *before* negotiation can be acceptable. Every other kind of move will be taken for bluff or treachery—and very likely will be.

The other hope is that the situation at home becomes so delicate that America will not be able to afford the Vietnam war. The consequences of her *laissez-faire* attitude to planning are variously disastrous. Besides the derelict state of her education, such things as her production rates and her infant mortality rates are nothing to be proud of: they are behind those of many European nations. The racial problem is (with every reason to be) explosive. Indeed, this weakness of America at home makes Labour's treachery even more craven: America is very sensitive, and a little of the only treatment she respects—tough handling—might well provoke an internal regeneration by a healthy shock to American arrogance and complacency—which is our only hope.

Vyvyan Holland

I find the questions, as they are put, are not easy to answer, especially as you require "brief answers."

Therefore, I will put the questions in another form, so that I can answer them.

1. Am I in favor of Chinese Communistic infiltration into North Vietnam, with a view to the spread of communism to that country? Answer, No.

2. Do I believe that, in the event of Vietnam becoming Communist, it will stop there? Answer, No.

3. Do I think that, in the event of China succeeding in communizing Vietnam, Australia would be the next objective? Answer, Yes.

4. Do the Australians also think the menace of Chinese communism is one to be feared, and is that why they are sending troops to Vietnam? Answer, Yes.

I can now answer your questions. If the only way to stop the spread of communism in the East is intervention by the United States, then, unfortunately, I am for it.

As far as the second question is concerned, the conflict is insoluble. It is a clash of ideologies, and so long as China continues to support the North Vietnamese, I cannot see how the problem can be resolved.

Elspeth Huxley

In Vietnam, the issues seem to me too complicated to be just "for" or "against" US intervention. This intervention was launched in good faith as an attempt to contain communism as a political force and prevent the Chinese domination of the whole of Asia, including Malaysia and India. If you believe, as most Americans do, in democracy as good in itself, and communism enforced by a foreign and imperialist power as an evil, then they were right to try to contain communism in Asia. The fact that they chose Vietnam to make their stand is another matter. Probably this decision was influenced by two considerations: the general retrospective belief that "we"—the forces of democracy, I suppose—made a profound mistake in not containing the forces of Nazism originally on the Rhine, and later in Czechoslovakia, instead of appeasing and giving way until the invasion of Poland; and the success of the UN operation in Korea in arresting the onward march of Chinese communism.

That they made a miscalculation is now abundantly clear. This is not a question of moral rightness or wrongness; it is a question of strategy. The whole thing has become a disaster. Obviously, the sooner they can extricate themselves from Vietnam the better. But how can they? Here I can't go along with the people who sign manifestos about the need to negotiate, etc., with Vietcong. It is to the leaders of Vietcong, and of China, that these appeals should be addressed, not to

President Johnson. And with what results? Just about as much as throwing a handful of peanuts at a nuclear power station. The opposition want to win, not to negotiate. They are ambitious, ruthless and determined, and they mean to dominate Asia, possibly the world. Lots of people have wanted this before them, and others will again—there is nothing new in the power struggle. One of the profound mistakes British and other liberals make is to assume that other people, in other lands, *want* peace and abhor war and suffering; so when there are no peaceful settlements, the fault is always "ours." If the rulers of the peoples in these other lands, such as China, could get all they want without war, perhaps they would, but they certainly don't shrink from war if that appears to be necessary. In fact they probably welcome it as a form of military maneuver, trying out new weapons, building up a cadre of experienced fighters, practice in tactics and so on, just as both Germans and Russians welcomed the Spanish Civil War as a practice ground for bigger things.

So I think it probably becomes a question of deciding whether to pull out of Vietnam completely with a tremendous loss of face, and a pretty shattering effect on the morale of the Americans themselves, and abandon Asia to the Chinese Communists, and choosing another line to make a stand; or whether to continue the present war with all its beastliness, futility and inevitably increasing weight. On this I share none of the responsibility and would not presume to offer President Johnson and the Americans the benefit of uninformed advice. Of course they should "explore every avenue," and I personally think they will probably have to pull out in the end. That they have made a mistake is clear and I expect they know it. And I am sure there are a lot of boneheaded, fire-eating generals about who are a menace. But I think the Americans will, must and can deal with this themselves. As we have not got a single man ourselves involved in Vietnam, I think to tell them what they ought to do can only irritate or even infuriate most Americans. Which comes back to the fact that, because my trade is that of writing books, I do not think that qualifies me to tell the Americans what they ought to do. We are all involved in the long run, of course, and entitled to opinions. But not necessarily to preach them to others.

Hammond Innes

There is no point in considering whether the Americans should intervene—they have. They see Vietnam as part of the struggle to contain communism. The similarities with Korea are obvious, but this time China bides her time. Her people are very industrious, very clever. They have spread their business tentacles throughout Southeast Asia. In such a situation China does not need to go to war. She just needs patience, and as a race the Chinese are supposed to have more patience than the Americans. Such an observation does not point to the means of resolving the conflict, only to what may ultimately happen. And, as always, it is the people, struggling to exist in a shattered country—the fighting men, too—who have to pay for the political stupidities that have allowed this creeping war to escalate.

Pamela Hansford Johnson

I am against the intervention of the United States in Vietnam, which is causing an infinity of suffering, and can leave only a legacy of shame affecting the whole of the Western world. "This is not Munich, but Spain."

To pretend that a solution is easy would be naïve. The first thing to be done is to stop the bombing, the napalm-throwing, and the poisoning of crops (i.e., the destruction of a poor nation's food by the technological devices of a rich nation) instantly. Then everything must be done to try to reconvene the Geneva Convention of 1954.

Uwe Johnson

Some good people do not tire of declaring in public that they abominate their country's participation in the war in Vietnam; what can they have in mind? The good people claim for themselves the observation that war is no longer permitted between civilized nation-states; the good people stood pat when the colonial policy of civilized nation-states disturbed those people merely with police, before they could become an independent nation. The good people are heard complaining that the world's greatest country uses advanced weapon systems against a small country, partly experimentally, and especially the trying out of more effective means of annihilation irritates the good people; the good people sat quietly in the corner while the armies gained capacity; they granted the military the very diet of maneuvers; now they scream over the machine's natural greed for fodder truer to life. The good people dwell on morals; observance of the Geneva Agreements is what they wish, negotiations, fair elections, withdrawal of foreign troops, decency, they say, and the Dignity of Man; they talk to the superhuman egoism of a state as to a private person with private virtues. What the good people do not like about the war is that it is visible; the good people eat of the fruits their Governments harvest for them in Asian politics and on Asian markets. The good people want a good capitalism, an abstention from expansion by war; the good people want a singing horse—what they do not want is communism. The good people want a good world; they do nothing about it. The good people do not try to stop the workers from earning their living by production of armaments; they do not hold up the conscripted who risk their lives in this war; the good people stand in the marketplace and point themselves out as the better ones. These good people will soon, with embarrassment, describe their protests against this war as their juvenile period, as the good people before them now talk about Hiroshima and democracy and Cuba. The good people should kindly shut up. Let them be good to their kids, even to kids who are not their own, to their cats, even to strange ones. If only they would stop talking about a species of goodness they help to make impossible.

James Jones

1. Against. Under present limitations it is impossible for the US to *win* this war. Strategically and tactically the US is fighting from an untenable position. To invade North Vietnam would be to engage ourselves in a major war that the entire world can ill afford at the moment. If we did "win" this limited war I doubt if we could enforce "free elections" which the Vietcong would not be able to "fix." The entire operation appears to me to be a lost cause, and I agree with Walter Lippmann that we must learn that this is not an ideological war but a war of the Asians to rid themselves of domination by the Western white man. Morally I am against the bombing of North Vietnam; but then I am morally against the terrorism, torture, indiscriminate shooting, fear control and impressment of the peasants by the Vietcong and North Vietnamese. I am totally cynical about the Vietcong, North Vietnamese and Red Chinese. I cannot agree with the dewy-eyed idealists who believe the Red Chinese and their satellites will leave us alone for the next fifty years if we withdraw from Vietnam and Thailand. But I do believe that there are civilizing elements at work in China as well as in the other Asian countries. And only if left alone by us Western white men can they hope to influence or prevail. Meanwhile, the spot we have picked to make our "fight" or "stand" simply is not a tenable one. If the US got out of Vietnam today, I am convinced that within three years or four a united Communist Vietnam would be, if not in a war, in a basic and major argument with their hereditary enemies, the Chinese.

Then we could sit back and let the Chinese embassies get stoned.

2. By total US withdrawal, which means Thailand also. But this is a difficult problem, militarily. First we should cease the bombing. This means that the re-enforcement from North Vietnam could proceed apace, and I have no doubt that it would! If we cease our "search and destroy" missions, which effectively keep the enemy off balance, he would be free to come in close and lob mortars into just about everywhere in our "coastal enclaves." But this is basically a military problem, and in the end the decision here has to be political. I think the North Vietnamese have suffered enough by now that they would probably allow us to do this without using the military advantages we would be giving them. At any rate, we would find out—the world would find out—just how much "good faith" exists on the *other* side. With all this in mind, I think we should first of all cease the bombing, then let it be known we are willing to withdraw if allowed to, and if allowed to, I think we should begin withdrawal of all our enormous and expensive military installations in both Vietnam and Thailand. Then we should let Red China into the UN, and begin the long and probably arduous process of civilizing them.

Stanley Kauffmann

Question 1 seems dated and inadequate. One can no longer rationally oppose the US intervention in Vietnam because one can no longer rationally hope for US withdrawal, however right in principle such withdrawal might be. Each US mistake has been (thinly) masked by a larger succeeding mistake, which claims its antecedent as justification with a horrible kind of illogical logic, until now the way back is blocked. I have only two hopes in this matter: I hope the US Government will stop deceiving the American people, even out of good motives. I hope the US Government will not extend the war.

As to Question 2: I don't know the answer and can't see that anyone else does. I have read dozens of plans, from Lord Avon's * up and down, and think they are all basically senseless because eventually all depend on the cooperation of Hanoi (not visible) and on the maintenance of a status arrived at by treaty (not prob-

* In his book *Towards Peace in Indochina* (Boston and London, 1966), Lord Avon suggested that the Geneva Agreements of 1954 should be regarded as still valid. The machinery for their implementation might be refurbished, and the Control Commission given extended powers; Indochina would thus be neutralized and the supply of arms to countries in the area prevented. —Eds.

able). I think one can appeal only to time. The tangle is by now too complex to be unraveled; therefore it should be frozen—battle lines should be maintained as close to what they are now as is possible, for as long as possible—for years if necessary—to allow changes to take place internally within all the parties to the matter. Governments, temperaments, tempers can change radically in five or ten years (see Yugoslavia and the USSR). If some kind of relatively stable armed state can be maintained—an American occupation of South Vietnam (that includes economic aid)—then perhaps the attritions and increments of time will bring changes on all sides that make *rapprochement* possible.

I know this is a wan possibility. I hope that someone suggests and expedites a sounder plan, but as yet I know of none. At present I see no alternative to an armed and inevitably blood-spotted wait other than a growing and potentially cataclysmic war.

Walter Kaufmann

The US military intervention in Vietnam was a great blunder from the start and has been escalated into a moral outrage. The intention was presumably to apply the lessons of Munich and Korea; but the analogy with Munich is misleading, and in Korea the United States was "deputized by the United Nations to repel the aggressor in its name." The Lawyers Committee on American Policy Toward Vietnam has argued persuasively that US military intervention in Vietnam violates the charter of the UN as well as the Geneva Agreements of 1954, and that "the intensity and destructiveness of United States warfare in Vietnam is contrary to international law." (These quotations come from Section 4 of *The New York Times,* Sunday, January 15, 1967, p. E9.)

The intellectual and moral shortcomings of US policy have a common source: the extreme self-righteousness of our leading foreign policy makers blinds them to the thoughts, feelings, and humanity of their opponents in Vietnam. Least of all are our leaders able to see themselves and their policies as they appear to their enemies and, alas, to much of the world. This blindness, which is shared by most Americans, can be readily illustrated by a striking example.

When Israel made a raid on a Jordanian village in November 1966, she was quickly condemned by the American Government, press, and public; and while I have no wish whatever to defend this raid, these condemnations were instances of hypocrisy, self-righteousness, and an insistence on judging other nations by one standard, the United States by another.

A few years ago most Americans considered it intolerable to have a hostile Government "only 90 miles" from our shores, and an attempt was actually made to topple it by force. If our direct neighbors were pledged to destroy the US and American lives were lost constantly to infiltrators from across the border, would we complain to the UN or take the law into our own hands? And if the UN refused to condemn such attacks on us—as it did in the case of attacks on Israel—would we continue to forbear? And would we be content to accept it as a commonplace that we differ from other people by being the sort who allow themselves to be killed like sheep, without fighting back?

While we were condemning Israel, we were fighting a war half the way around the world, ostensibly to prove that aggression does not pay. And we keep being told that Americans killed, while they are napalm-bombing Vietnamese villages, are dying for our security. But Israel's raid is said to have exceeded the provocation.

I am less concerned to plead extenuating circumstances for Israel, whose raid I did not applaud, than to suggest that our Government, press, and public should learn to see themselves as they see others, and as others see us.

Our current intervention is not on behalf of the UN. Rather we are demonstrating our faith in an appalling double standard: What is considered criminal when a small nation does it on a small scale is considered a service to world morality when done on a vast scale by the US. The logic and ethics our Government invokes to justify its bombings would not only justify North Vietnam, as well as any other country asked to do so by Hanoi, if they bombed the US: if it were generally accepted it would introduce havoc and reduce humanity to barbarism.

Our leaders see themselves as the guardians of humanity. In fact, they demonstrate that the ancient Greeks were wise when they did not distinguish as sharply as we usually do between moral and intellectual failure. Scholars still debate whether the "flaw" that so often precipitates tragedy is an error in judgment or a moral shortcoming. The mode of our intervention and our bombings show how inseparable both can be, and how difficult it is to wake from blindness before tragedy has run its full course.

Yuri Kazakov *

Although innumerable protests of every kind from people all over the world against American aggression in Vietnam apparently do not reach the ears of the

American Government, and consequently so far appear in vain, I consider that writers must protest even more actively, even louder.

I believe that American aggression in Vietnam is a crime against humanity.

When in a distant country one half of a nation incites the other half, and hundreds of thousands of young Americans cross the ocean in order to kill and be killed; when napalm and all kinds of other bombs are dropped on bamboo villages, and instead of rolling up their sleeves and setting to work to make life better on earth, young Americans shoot, hang, and burn; when they, on the orders of their Government, do the same things the Germans did on our soil and on the soil of Europe just over twenty years ago; then the President and his advisers are lying when they call in vain for the blessing of Almighty God; pastors are lying when they pray for the victory of American arms. And the generals, the journalists, and the politicians are lying when they pride themselves on "genuine democracy" in their country, because when a democracy commits evil it ceases to be a democracy.

Yet in spite of everything, I believe in the power of the word, in the power of honest and courageous words, because defined by words, any event receives its true evaluation. At times the word is powerless to stop evil, because the writer is not in a position of power; the writer cannot give orders and cannot stop bloodshed. But with words, the writer can brand each wicked action, even when that wicked and dirty deed is victorious.

Thirty years ago in the Spanish Civil War the Franco regime was triumphant, but the greatest writers of the time, including Americans, commented honestly and loudly on this regime. The regime received the name of Fascism, and however long Franco rules, he is already defined by a word; he is a Fascist. His Government has already been assessed by history. It had received its evaluation even before it came to power.

I am firmly convinced that in just the same way the actions of the present American Government will find, indeed already have found, their proper evaluation in the protests of all nations.

Frank Kermode

I am against the American intervention, believing that it should not have been started; and of course I am against escalation, though it seems useless to pretend that there could be one without the other, or that it is now within the power of the US Government to refrain from escalation. Somebody else has got to get the Americans out; short of an unimaginable disaster this will of course happen, and it is hard to see by whose agency it will happen if not by that of the USSR. Meanwhile the important jobs are to persuade the Russians to act sooner rather than later, and the Americans to escalate as slowly as possible. The worldwide movement for peace in Vietnam helps, and would help more if it occasionally attended to the difficulty of the American position and the severe limitations on American freedom of choice.

Bernard Kops

I am against the American intervention in Vietnam because I do not want the world to commit suicide. No one can win this war and everyone must lose. Vietnam is *us*. There is only *us* left in this world. When Vietnamese cities are bombed we are also destroying ourselves. But I have no idea how the conflict can be resolved.

Jerzy Kosinski

The simplest answer to the two questions is to state that I am against any intervention in Vietnam, and that the resolution of the conflict should be sought through the international peacemaking bodies. However, I cannot propose such answers because the human record proves them to be largely ineffective.

Much of my own life, together with that of the two remaining members of my once numerous family, has been and still is influenced by interventions and oppressions of various types. Major among these was World War II: a conflict not yet resolved. Final terms and accepted borders have not been produced by the peacemakers and the conflict continues.

Mankind has not yet developed any workable way of solving its conflicts; indeed, conflict itself is the accepted foundation of our morality as any part of human experience will testify.

Signing petitions, answering questions, and making pronouncements only encourages further conflicts over the solutions we tender for existing disagreements. Intervention is an uncertain weapon; at best it can succeed only while actual, and more often strengthens the course of action it attempts to terminate. Peace is an uncertain compromise; it exists only by agreement while the necessary reshaping of conflict and regrouping of forces are achieved.

Mark Lane

1. Of course I oppose the intervention of any nation in the affairs of another. It is illegal. In Vietnam the American presence violates the Charter of the United Nations and any number of treaties to which the United States was a signatory. The *conduct* of the armed forces, in addition to its very presence, is in further violation of sacred treaty obligations. The use of napalm and explosives against civilians, the torture and murder of prisoners, the use of chemicals are all proscribed by treaties. But here I speak with the discipline of my other profession, law, and you asked my opinion as an author. I am against the war because my country seeks to destroy a philosophy and genuine aspirations for national independence with guns. It cannot be done. Not now, not ever. Do not these words constitute aid and comfort to the enemy? I recognize no enemy in Vietnam. The enemy of world peace lives not in the jungle but in the large white houses with quiet cool lawns where he has always lived. And in the unlikely instance that these words should reach Vietnam let them be proof that there are some born here who wish them no harm and who oppose with all their hearts the immoral and dirty war waged by this mighty Administration against a suffering people.

2. There is but one way out of Vietnam. Out. Now and unconditionally. Should this bring about the establishment of another Communist state, that is a choice that must be left to the people of Vietnam. Better that they live with their own choice than die by ours.

Marghanita Laski

Over past years I've been reluctantly brought to conclude that American intervention anywhere is largely harmful. It sounds grossly arrogant to say that their levels—in culture, in sensitivity, in intelligence—are, broadly speaking, too low for the responsibilities they assume, but, with rare exceptions, I fearfully think this is the case. Leaving aside the often gratuitous cruelty of the Vietnam war, the sheer political foolishness of white intervention in Asia at this moment is arrogantly, appallingly lacking in respect to Asian capacity and potential, and harmful to us all.

How it should end I don't know. But a gesture of humility, an admission of error by the Americans, would lead one to respect them as nothing else could.

Doris Lessing

This war should be stopped at once, and by any means. That it is totally destructive for the Vietnamese seems not to need saying, even if a major war is not precipitated by it, which seems terribly likely. What is not said often enough is that the war is demoralizing for the United States, and for Britain insofar as we support the United States. Ten years ago I would not have believed it possible that France would be the nation, rather than Britain, with the guts to say "no" to America—but so it has turned out. As for the United States' claim that they are containing communism, what they are in fact doing is to deepen cynicism everywhere about democracy and the values we purport to uphold. To take just one part of the world, Africa—what sort of effect can it have there, watching the contempt for human life, the casual bloody-mindedness with which the United States conducts this war?

What means should be used to stop it? As a start Britain should withdraw all support, of any kind. Until then we have no right to tell other people what to do.

Denise Levertov

I am absolutely opposed to the US war of aggression in Vietnam. Not only is it an unjustifiable interference hypocritically carried on in the name of "freedom" while in fact its purpose is to further the strategic ends of a Government whose enormous power has destroyed the morality of its members; but it is being waged by means of atrocities. This is a war in which more children are being killed and maimed than fighting men. Napalm, white phosphorus, fragmentation bombs, all used deliberately on a civilian population; poisoning of crops, defoliation of forests; not to speak of the horrendous blight of disease and famine that follows, the corruption, prostitution, and every kind of physical and moral suffering—nothing whatsoever could possibly justify these crimes.

Violence always breeds more violence and is never a solution even when it temporarily seems to be. Violence of this magnitude, even if the ultimate holocaust it is swiftly leading to is averted—i.e., if we at least stop in time to avoid a still larger war—promises a dreadful future for America, full of people tortured and distorted with the knowledge (conscious or unconscious) of what we have done. One does not need to be a bomber pilot to feel this; one need only be an American who did nothing to stop the war, or not enough; one has only to be a human being. It is hard to be an artist in this time because it is hard to be human: in the dull ever-accumulating horror of the war news it is more difficult each day to keep remembering the creative and joyful potential of human beings, and to fulfill that potential in one's own life, as testimony. Shame, despair, disgust, these are the reverberations that threaten to silence poets thousands of miles away from where the bombs are falling. The struggle of all artists and all pacifists is to overcome their nausea and actively hold to what their work has caused them to know—the possibility of beautiful life.

I believe that cessation of all violence and withdrawal of all troops from Vietnam is the only right action for the US. I would like to see this withdrawal followed by the penitent presentation to the people of Vietnam by the US of huge quantities of food and supplies—such quantities that people here would feel the pinch, actually sacrifice something, not merely donate a surplus. I would like to see this given absolutely outright, and unaccompanied by US "advisers," though large numbers of doctors, nurses, and other people who might really be of use in reconstructing the ravaged country might humbly offer their services to work under Vietnamese supervision. Such acts of penitence, distinct from the guilt that stews in its own juice, would do something to make the future more livable for our children.

Jakov Lind

Cancer. Car accidents. Coronaries. Weather. Rats. Ordinary life. All very deadly. The free West—the enslaved East. Outdated phrases. There is freedom for some, slavery for others, here and there.

Fighting partisans and destroying villages and their inhabitants, because most of the Vietnamese seem to prefer to go Communist, is stupid, immoral, nauseating.

The war in Vietnam is the ultimate in stupidity, for which there has never been an ultimate solution. Why not try a shrewd solution to combat Communists in Asia? Help them to get to power; sooner or later they will all turn revisionist. America is missing a historic chance, there may be no second one. Let's remember

H-bombs have their use to keep the peace, in wartime they are useless. This war is ridiculous and criminal because it fights no cause at all. In ten years' time the United States would be grateful for any friend; moderate Communists are America's best friends. Why turn them into fanatic enemies?

Poor, blinded America.

Eric Linklater

In the summer of 1951 I was in Korea. The beginning of that war had been the sudden invasion of South Korea by the Communist North and the almost simultaneous announcement, by the North, that its action had been necessary to counter aggression from the South. The small expeditionary force that Britain was able to send in defense of the South consisted, at first, of a battalion of the Middlesex Regiment, another of the Argylls. I had talked with their survivors, whose memories of the war were dominated by the appalling misery of the refugees who had fled from the North.

The North pretended to be the aggrieved and virtuous party, but a multitude of starving, half-frozen refugees chose to escape from its virtue. There were no fugitives *to* the North.

Today, in Vietnam, there is a comparable situation. The Communists were the original aggressors, and there has been strenuous propaganda to persuade the world that blame lies on the United States. In South Vietnam there are, perhaps, a million refugees from North Vietnam. The refugee tide, that is, has run in the same direction as in Korea: from the North to the South. It is not unreasonable to suppose that there, as in Korea, the refugees know more about Asian communism, its aims and methods, than many well-intentioned people whose opinions are so deeply influenced by their detestation of war as to blind them to its causes.

One must ask what would happen if the President of the United States decided to pull out from Vietnam; and the immediate answer is that the refugees from North Vietnam, and the soldiers of South Vietnam, would be left to the mercy of the Northern Communists, and communism has nowhere been identified with compassion. The secondary answer is that all the adjacent countries of Southeast Asia would then lie open to Communist attack, and as Communist policy is openly expansionist, they would certainly be attacked when, in Communist eyes, the time was ripe for further aggression.

In that event Britain would be called on to acknowledge its obligations to SEATO, and reluctantly we would be forced to admit our indebtedness to the United States for previously having fought a war that was waged in our interest as much as in support of the hazardous cause of democracy in Saigon.

The Communist North has been given every opportunity to discuss peace terms, and refused all invitations to negotiate. The Americans declared peace in the air, and for several weeks, while their bombers lay inactive, the North Vietnamese regrouped and reinforced their army: They took advantage of a truce to prepare renewal of the war, precisely as the North Koreans had done in 1952.

There is no one, with any atom of sense or scrap of sensibility, who does not deplore the frightful facts of war. I have seen something of the destruction done in three wars, but also I have seen, in Italy and Korea, the tidal stream of refugees, and that stream always sets away from the fear imposed by initial aggression. And a Communist triumph in Vietnam would presently start other tidal streams, of wretchedness and terror, throughout Southeast Asia.

In the preface to *Her Privates We*—one of the memorable novels of the First World War—its anonymous author wrote: "War is waged by men; not by beasts, or by gods. It is a peculiarly human activity. To call it a crime against mankind is to miss at least half its significance; it is also the punishment of a crime. That raises a moral question, the kind of problem with which the present age is disinclined to deal."

It is a problem which most of us, in this age, are still inclined to shirk. But the President of the United States is facing it squarely, and despite the agony of mind to which he has admitted, he has faced it with faith in man's ability to judge right from wrong, and with determination that wrong shall not prosper and enlarge its capacity for wrongdoing.

Richard Llewellyn

I am wholeheartedly in favor of the United States of America, and I believe that President Johnson's decision to support South Vietnam, at the time he did, saved the rest of the world from destruction. The ruffians governing Communist China have no conscience in any sense of the term. The undisciplined brutes infesting the streets of China today and making ordinary people's lives a misery are only one result of government for ruffians, by ruffians; and when those ruffians

are able to use nuclear power, we need expect neither warning nor mercy.

The conflict in Vietnam will be settled only when China—that is to say, ruffianly China—as opposed to the vast majority of the Chinese people on the mainland—at one time, possibly the most naturally pacific nation on earth—is taught the lesson of superior power, rational thinking, and a proper regard for the rights of Everyman. By superior power, I mean by air and sea, of necessity nuclear; by rational thinking, I mean a return to the decencies of diplomatic and commercial exchange and the liberation of artists and scientists; and by a proper regard for the rights of Everyman, I mean those, all of them, incorporated in the Charter of the United Nations, whether immanent or tacit.

Colin MacInnes

The French have an annoying way of answering any apparently simple question by saying it is "wrongly formulated." This would, however, seem to me to be the only possible answer to your first question, since the real one surely is, "Are you for, or against, the intervention of *any* people in the territory and affairs of another?"

Thus, one cannot consider US intervention in Vietnam without also considering, for instance, that of the USSR in the Baltic states, of China in Tibet, of France in the Pacific Islands, of England in Rhodesia, and so on. The fact that fighting is taking place in the first case, and has ceased to, or has not yet, in the others, does not affect the principle of whether such intervention is ever justifiable anywhere.

One may also raise the question as to whether the intervention of the United States in their own territory is justifiable, since this intervention has resulted in the decimation and oppression of its original inhabitants, the Amerindians, and the subjection of such ethnic minorities as the American Negroes and Mexicans.

As to the second question, the conflict in Vietnam will clearly only be *resolved* both when all foreign intervention from whatever source ceases, and when the Vietnamese themselves reject the probable alternative of civil war.

I would add I think it highly unlikely that *all* such interventions will ever cease throughout the world until and unless nationalism, and racialism, and vast concentrations of economic power (whether capitalist or Marxist) are found by mankind to be the perilous wasteful frauds they are.

Marshall McLuhan

The answer to the first question depends upon how we recognize the role of the war in Westernizing the Orient. As a crash program of Westernization and education, the war consists in initiating the East in the mechanical technology of the industrial age. All would change if we were to use the technology of this century. In short, the answer to the first question in terms of war as an educational program suggests an area of discussion that has not been tapped. Perhaps any technological gap tends to be a major cause of war, even as it tends to be liquidated by education.

Do we not tend to regard war as conducted by means of the older technology as relatively endurable? What light does this throw on our own uses of the latest technology in relation to education?

Salvador de Madariaga

Who remembers now the peace campaign? It was loud, worldwide and admirably organized. It fought valiantly for peace during the time when the United States held the monopoly of nuclear power; and as soon as the Soviet Union became a nuclear power itself, the campaign petered out. Since then, there have been one or two rattlings of nuclear weapons on the part of the Soviet Union, which did not sound exactly peace-loving.

Nowadays, what gets painted on the walls is not PEACE or BAN THE BOMB, but PEACE IN VIETNAM. The Americans no longer spread microbes, as in Korea, but LBJ, HOW MANY KIDS HAVE YOU KILLED TODAY? The psychological strings are just as ably woven to pull at people's hearts.

The campaign is valiantly fought by two quite different battalions: the idealists, who hate the war in Vietnam because it is war; and the realists, who hate the war in Vietnam because it is in Vietnam. The former want an end to all war. The latter want to carry on the war beyond Vietnam, further out of the Communist world and further within that part of the world which is still free.

Hence the key difficulty: *There is no solution to the problem.* There are two reasons for this: the first is that there is no common aim; for the USA wants to clear out without opening the gates of both hot and cold Communist aggression, a flood that would engulf the rest of Southeast Asia plus Australia and New Zealand; while such is precisely the purpose of the Russians and of the Chinese (much as they may quarrel about tactics); and the second reason is that there is no guarantee whatever that the agreement, if arrived at, would be respected by the Communists. Witness the treatment of Maleter and Nagy exactly ten years ago, when the men at present in power in the Soviet Union were already powerful and responsible for the behavior of the USSR—to say nothing of the numberless cases of plain, downright betrayal by the Soviet Union under Stalin.

Norman Mailer

The truth is, maybe we need a war. It may be the last of the tonics. From Lydia Pinkham to Vietnam in sixty years, or bust. We're the greatest country ever lived for speeding up the time. So, let's do it right. Let's cease all serious wars, kids. Let's leave Asia to the Asians. Let us, instead, have wars which are like happenings. Let us have them every summer. Let us buy a tract of land in the Amazon, two hundred million acres will do, and throw in Marines and Seabees and Air Force, Scuba divers for the river bottom, motor-cyclists for the mud-races, carrier pilots landing on bounce-all decks in typhoons, invite them all, the Chinks and the Aussies, the Frogs and the Gooks and the Wogs, the Wops and the Russkies, the Yugos, the Israelis, the Hindus, the Pakistanis. We'll have war games with real bullets and real flamethrowers, real hot-wire correspondents on the spot, TV with phone-in audience participation, amateur war movie film contests for the soldiers, discotheques, Playboy Clubs, pictures of the corpses for pay TV, you know what I mean—let's get the hair on the toast for breakfast. So a write-in campaign (all of us) to King Corporation Exec Mr. Pres; let us tell him to get the boys back home by Christmas, back from Vietnam and up the Amazon for summer. Yours—readers—till the next happening.

Unless Vietnam is the happening. Could that be? Could that really be? Little old Vietnam just a happening? Cause if it is, Daddy Warbucks, couldn't we have the happening just with the Marines and skip all that indiscriminate roast tit and naked lunch, all those bombed-out civilian ovaries, Mr. J., Mr. LBJ, Boss Man of Show Biz—I salute you in your White House Oval; I mean America will shoot all over the shithouse wall if this jazz goes on, Jim.

Olivia Manning

Yes; and against the intervention of any non-Vietnamese force. The American complaint that North Vietnam will not negotiate a peace seems to me disingenuous. Why should they negotiate with an invader against whom they can more than hold their own? Fear that withdrawal of American troops would result in occupation by other foreign troops is probably unjustified. If North Vietnam can resist occupation by a major power like the United States, they can resist a much weaker power, such as Communist China. This is a pro-American attitude as the majority of US citizens are, for one reason or another, against the war.

The Fulbright proposals are excellent as far as they go: (1) cessation of bombing in North Vietnam; (2) National Liberation Front to be included in negotiations; (3) free elections; (4) international aid for the desolated areas.

To this I would add the withdrawal from the whole of Vietnam of all non-Vietnamese forces to enable Vietnam to work out her own destiny as America did after the Declaration of Independence. I also see need to compensate those of the Vietnamese people who have suffered injury and loss as a result of foreign intervention in their domestic affairs.

Herbert Marcuse

1. The intervention in Vietnam has, in my opinion, turned, not into a war but into a crime against humanity. The question whether or not I am in favor of such intervention is therefore preposterous.

2. I think that the solution to the conflict lies in the withdrawal of all foreign troops from Vietnam. The setting up of a neutral international police force would assure the protection of persons likely to be subjected to terroristic retaliation. Those Vietnamese most conspicuously identified with the American intervention will probably prefer to leave the country; they are not likely to encounter great difficulties in finding political asylum.

Kingsley Martin

I am completely against United States intervention in Vietnam. Apart from the war's horrifying cruelty, it increases the strength of communism in Asia and makes world war more likely. Left alone, Ho Chi Minh would come less under Chinese influence than he does today and the chances are that Vietnam would stand in relation to Peking as Tito's Yugoslavia does to Moscow.

It would be best if the United States left Vietnam altogether, but to demand that is not realistic. The hawks in America regard the war against the Vietcong as a round in an inevitable war with China. If we can get a settlement that forces them to accept a division of Vietnam, similar to that in Korea, I suppose that is the best we can now look for. I hope the Russians agree to press for a recall of the Geneva Conference, and in that case, that both America and Hanoi might be compelled to negotiate.

Gavin Maxwell

I cannot see the Vietnam war in any isolated context; the questions posed might equally be applied to any war in historical times. I start with my own postulation that there can be no aggression between members of the same species without the presence of fear in the widest sense of the word. Man is the most aggressive of all animal species, and it follows that his fears are infinitely more numerous and diverse than those of any other mammal.

This war is a war of fear and consequent aggression on both sides. Caught between them are the indigenous people—the only players to whom I respond subjectively. The present indigenous "governmental" personnel do not appear to me to merit consideration.

Intervention by the USA would have been justified only if (1) it had been to arrest the spread of a wholly destructive ideology such as Hitler's (debatable); and (2) if this intervention had reasonable prospect of success (even more debatable).

How this or any other such conflict should be resolved poses gigantic questions. Even assuming that (1) above cannot be supported, unconditional withdrawal of the USA from South Vietnam would inevitably lead to unthinkable reprisals by the Vietcong on the allegedly "collaborationist" South Vietnamese. In all probability the Vietcong would not tolerate the presence of independent observers after US withdrawal. It would, I imagine, be impossible for the USA to evacuate the entire South Vietnam population prior to withdrawal—which might otherwise have seemed the only solution.

As I have not enough world political knowledge to assess the strategic bone over which the dogs are fighting, I can only suggest a gradual and planned reduction of fear to reduce the degree of aggression. The implementation of this suggestion calls for detailed and specific knowledge that I do not possess. Presumably some sections of the active parties do.

Thomas Merton

I might preface these remarks by saying that I am no no longer a very enthusiastic side-taker. For instance in the US Presidential election of 1964 along with the majority of voters I took the side of Lyndon Johnson against Barry Goldwater, and my reason for doing so was that I did not want Goldwater's belligerent policy in Vietnam. However, though Johnson won the election, Goldwater's policy in Vietnam was what we got. The taking of sides, politically, may not always be a useful or significant exercise. But it may nevertheless remain morally necessary.

In my opinion the exorbitant US war effort in Vietnam cannot be explained or justified by the reasons that are officially given ("to prevent South Vietnam from being overrun by communism from the North"). The game of escalation continues to be more and more aggressive. Why is the US anxious to maintain such huge military bases in Southeast Asia? Are these necessary for the "defense" of South Vietnam?

No matter what side we may have taken in 1937, World War II was prepared in Spain by the great belligerents. It was their training field and the proving ground for their new weapons. Who suffered most cruelly? The innocent, the defenseless, the unarmed. Who gained by it? Not Spain. The same can be said of Vietnam today.

Therefore when I take a side in this question, it is not the side of the United States and it is not the side of communism. Both Peking and Washington want the war to go on. I am on the side of the people who are being burned, cut to pieces, tortured, held as hostages, gassed, ruined, destroyed. They are the victims of both sides. To take sides with massive power is to take sides against the innocent. The side I take is, then, the side of the people who are sick of war and want peace in order to rebuild their country.

Once this has been said, it must be admitted that the American policy of escalation is what makes peace and order impossible in Vietnam. As long as bombings continue in North Vietnam, as long as rumors of an invasion of North Vietnam continue to grow, it is useless to expect an end to the horrors and inhumanities of the war. Resistance and counter-escalation are the obvious result. US aggression must stop. The prob-

lems of South Vietnam must be settled by arbitration, and by the free unhampered action of the people of Vietnam themselves, not by force, by puppet dictatorship or by military might. The initiative must come from the US and must begin with de-escalation and a cessation of bombings in North Vietnam.

Can President Johnson understand this? Perhaps not. But in that case the responsibility for World War III may be found resting on his shoulders and on those of the US military-industrial complex which is the chief beneficiary of this callous and inhuman conflict. I, therefore, join with those who deplore it.

James A. Michener

Because I have served in the Southeast Asia area for many years, because I have lived in various parts of Vietnam and the surrounding countries, because I participated intimately in the war in Korea and less so in the war that the Philippines conducted against a guerrilla Communist assault, but primarily because I have served in Indonesia, Thailand, Burma, India, Ceylon and Pakistan, I am driven by experience of the past and concern for the future to support my Government's stand in Vietnam.

I believe that our stand in Korea some years ago helped to stabilize that part of the world. The agreement there reached was not a particularly good one, but it has worked. It has saved Japan, established a border zone that could be more or less controlled, and relieved international tensions that might otherwise have expanded into a world war. In Korea the United States learned it could of itself oppose both Russia and China, and that was a salutary discovery. But Russia and China also learned that they could not operate with impunity against world opinion. What may have been most important, Russia and China had a chance to see and to evaluate each other. On balance, I am not unhappy about our intervention in Korea.

I feel the same way about Vietnam. We have learned certain salutary facts and so have Russia and China. Again, perhaps the best outcome has been the chance for Russia and China to know one another better. I am not unhappy about our defense of South Vietnam. Much of my feeling stems however from my concern for the other nations in Asia listed above. That we have helped prevent a Communist aggression in Vietnam has strengthened their postures elsewhere. As the years pass, this will, I believe, be seen to have been the greatest positive outcome of the war, and it will minimize, I think, some of the deleterious results. Already we have seen positive results in the way in which Indonesia has resisted a Communist takeover.

But my deepest concern derives from an area and a problem which I have not yet mentioned. I have worked and studied for many years in both Australia and New Zealand and have concluded, rightly or wrongly, that they are the Pacific bastions of both the United States and Britain and indeed of much of Europe. If the reader is willing to say, "I don't care tuppence what happens to New Zealand and Australia," I cannot argue with him and this part of my reasoning will have little impression on him. But if he does care, if he does seek for this area some kind of reasonable stability, then he must, I think, wonder what would happen to these two free nations were all of Southeast Asia including Indonesia to go Communist.

My position is that if the United States were to have withdrawn from Vietnam two years ago, she would have had to move an equal amount of strength immediately into Australia, and the problems we had evaded in Vietnam would have now to be faced in Australia. I think that would have been a bad exchange, a very bad and insupportable exchange.

To my readers who have never been in this part of the world but who have strong moral feelings about the matter in the abstract, I will confess that on many points I agree with them, principally on the point that the time has now come when some kind of negotiated end must be put to this difficult war. After all, this is what we agreed to in Korea without loss of either position or honor and it is what we must agree to now. Therefore, I do not at all resent present peace pressures; in fact, I support them. The sooner peace can be attained, the better. This was my position in Korea. It is my opinion in Vietnam.

But the big point is that I am ready for peace precisely because the war so far has established certain basic principles that I have always supported in Asia, namely the fact that a Communist conspiracy must not be allowed to corrupt one free nation after another and subdue it. This fact has now been established; it may later have to be reiterated in other parts of the world. When I was in Russia recently I sensed a disposition on the part of Russian leaders to live with this basic fact, just as British and American leaders show a disposition to live with basic facts relating to Russia, and less so for the present but more so in future I trust, to live with such facts relating to China.

Because of my love for Asia, because of my concern over the remaining free states, because of my determination to do what I can to preserve a system of free nations, and especially because of my concern over the fate of New Zealand and Australia, I support my Government's position up to now in Vietnam . . . and I pray that it will do everything possible to terminate the affair as expeditiously as possible.

Arthur Miller

I was and am opposed to intervening in Vietnam, for political, military, and moral reasons. Prior to, and even after, our sending military "advisers," military leaders including Eisenhower and MacArthur warned against a land war in Asia, presumably because it was impossible to win against such immense masses of people and difficult terrain and communications.

Politically, it was clear from the beginning that, propaganda to the contrary notwithstanding, we were taking sides in a civil war; that while neither side represents what Americans consider democracy, our side had less claim even than the other to representing the majority or anything like it. At least Ho Chi Minh led the resistance to the Japanese and the French colonialists, while Marshal Ky is a mercenary fighter pilot whose last employment was gunning down Algerians fighting for their independence.

Without the people we are being driven to a "victory" which can only mean the devastation of the country and, above all, the destruction of peasants who have had nothing to say about their fate or their future. We are applying sheer brute force to a situation which is basically wanting in a political solution. This cannot and will not work and the proof is with us every day.

This war is a cancer spreading throughout international relations and into the economy and the spirit of the United States. It was a mistake to start with and blood is only committing us further to it.

I⁺ can be stopped. I cannot imagine a magic formula. If American forces ceased firing except to defend themselves where they stand, and ceased air bombing, and the truth of this got through to the other side, I believe an undeclared peace could begin to form.

Naomi Mitchison

I am, of course, against the intervention of the USA in Vietnam. But I am also against the intervention of China and I am not competent to disentangle the exact facts. These outside interferences and especially the American one have driven the country into a state of civil war, which is only too likely to go on even if all outside combatants walked out tomorrow. Civil wars are always the cruelest and seem to result in most deaths. It is quite clear that some of the worst horrors of this particular war are being perpetrated by Vietnamese on one another, with the concurrence of the United States Army. This war is meanwhile distracting opinion in America from consideration of any of the other pressing world problems and is diverting an incredible amount of money, which could be employed usefully and creatively, into useless destruction.

The French had to leave and so must the Americans. One hopes that the Vietnamese will then be able to settle their own affairs in their own way, though I am afraid this may not happen. There is bound to be a certain amount of retribution and punishment of people who have probably only been trying to save their own and their families' skins. But this war is so terribly bad for the whole world that it cannot be endured. It is lowering the general standards of decency and civilization and corrupting a whole generation of young men. Nothing can possibly make this worth while.

Communism is neither here nor there. Every country has the Communists which it deserves. Some day all this talk about communism will seem as crazy as the wars of religion only three hundred years ago. Manufacturing lies is almost as bad as torturing people.

Jessica Mitford

I think the intervention is unspeakably vile, and that the conflict should be resolved by total withdrawal of American forces from Vietnam. However, when I sent a telegram to that effect to the President, I got a letter back from the White House thanking me for my "message in support of the Administration's policies" in this hour of grave need for national unity. A simple mistake, no doubt; my telegram must have got put in the wrong pile. Yet this curious little incident served to heighten, for me, the nightmarish feeling that we are governed by deranged Dr. Strangeloves with whom communication is fast becoming impossible.

Nancy Mitford

I hate this horrible war and do not understand its motive; but it seems equally cruel and stupid whether it is fought to suppress communism or to bolster up Wall Street or both.

I would leave its solution to the only two living statesmen, U Thant and General de Gaulle.

Nicholas Monsarrat

When making declarations of opinion, an honest man should always declare his interest, and, if he is aware of it, his bias. My own bias is that I am pro-American.

Having lived fourteen years in Canada, with frequent visits to many part of the United States, I have come to think a great deal of the Americans as a people—a people still maliciously caricatured by the majority of British public opinion. It is true that a small minority of Americans are noisy boobs, in hideous flowered shirts, girt about with six cameras; just as a small minority of the British race expect nothing more from foreign travel than the privilege of being sick on the cobblestones of Calais.

The former are the Americans whom the British see, the latter are the British whom the French see. There is, or should be, a mutual understanding that these freaks are not representative.

Basically, the Americans are a sober, responsible, and informed people; and this is how we should think of them, when we are arguing about their presence in Vietnam.

The Americans are in Vietnam to discourage, to contain, and to outwit the advance of communism. This is something which we should certainly support, if we truly believe democracy to be superior to communism as a political goal, and if we wish to see it, at the very least, maintain its present areas of control. A glance at the map will show the alternative in the current arena of this contest: a southward march which will inevitably overrun all this area, and eventually submerge Australia and New Zealand.

These latter are our special friends and allies, and they have proved it throughout this century. It is now our turn to prove our friendship toward them. This is a debt of honor; and, if you don't believe in debts of honor, it is a smart stroke of self-interest as well. In a Communist world, Britain could not expect to be much more than a small outlying slum, assigned the task of producing its quota of plastic raincoats, stenciled "RAIN IS REVISIONIST! BE ON GUARD!"

The Americans, of course, are not fighting this war for us, nor for the Australians, nor for the New Zealanders. They are fighting it for America, just as we fought in two world wars for our own protection and survival. These are the facts of political life, and one need not disguise them. But this valiant struggle to contain communism is still our fight, and America is taking our share of the load, as well as her own, because we can no longer shoulder it ourselves.

We should not resent this. The people of the United States have not usurped our place in the world; they have succeeded to it, in a transfer of power of which we need not feel ashamed. We had a good run ourselves, and we did a good job. Naturally, it is sad that we can no longer police a democratic world-society; but in that regard our day is done, and our sun set. Now it is America's turn.

We should support her efforts loyally; and though she may strain this loyalty by baring the brutal face of war, it is still wrong to back away from that support. But whether we give support or not, one thing is certain: the Americans are there to stay until they win.

The contest itself can be solved only by agreement, which will involve on one side a tacit surrender. When the Communists discover that they have reached the limits of expansion, and can gain no more ground, they will call a halt, and go away. So will the Americans. This has been promised over and over again by President Johnson and his advisers, in unmistakable terms. He has said: "We want no US bases in Southeast Asia. We do not desire to retain US troops in South Vietnam after peace is assured. We will withdraw our soldiers once South Vietnam is securely guaranteed the right to shape its own future."

I believe him. The fact that he has rural tastes and a funny accent does not make him a liar. He, and the Americans, are fighting for the kind of world we believe in. When that fight is won, *then* we can afford the luxury of disdain. But not until then, and not now.

Luís de Sttau Monteiro

Military intervention in Vietnam should be stopped now at all costs. One can no longer be against colonialism in principle and for colonialism in practice.

How? The democratic way.

Send the generals home and use them for decorating the attic, or shut them in a room and let them kill each other—killing is all they are good at—but send them home.

Let the people choose what they want without anybody's interference. There are more things in heaven and earth than are dreamed of in any businessman's philosophy—and these are the things worth living for. If Vietnam's choice is not what the Americans would have made, so what? Who cares for what the Americans think is good for the Vietnamese? Not the Vietnamese, obviously, if they decided to pursue their own happiness instead of someone else's.

Marianne Moore

Does it *have* to be "Give me death or liberty"? It is shortsightedly irresponsible, I think, to permit Communist domination and acquiesce in the crushing of the weak by the strong. *Can* negotiation be imposed by force? Winston Churchill thought appeasement solved nothing.

Alan Moorehead

I have never been able to understand what the Americans are supposed to be doing in Vietnam. They do nothing but harm to themselves and everybody else. The Asians don't want them. Vietnam is an impossible terrain for military operations of this kind—as the French could have told them years ago. Even if they win they will never stop the spread of communism through Southeast Asia—which presumably was the prime object of their intervention.

If they are determined to have a military base in that part of the world why not fall back on northern Australia, a country where they would be welcome and secure? No one will think any the less of them if they do this; on the contrary they will be admired, whereas now they are hated.

Dom Moraes

I deplore American intervention in Vietnam. It has turned a small-scale and localized war into a large-scale war with unpredictable powers of expansion. It has propped up puppets in the South, and caused too many deaths to be thought of comfortably. The methods forced upon the Americans (napalm, the bombing of civilians) have been barbarous ones: this is a war even more barbarous than most.

The only way in which the deadlock can end is for the Americans to pull their troops out. Presumably this would mean that they admitted defeat, and presumably too South Vietnam would turn Communist thereafter. But that is a matter for the people of the country, and I imagine those Vietnamese who accepted the Americans would accept the Communists with equal alacrity or apathy. The only thing worth fighting for is peace.

Raymond Mortimer

Comments inspired by emotion without knowledge can have little value; and the suffering caused by the war in Vietnam horrifies me so profoundly that I cannot bear to read or think about it. That is shameful. But two visits in the 1950's to Southeast Asia left me with a particular liking for its varied peoples and their ways of life. Now the Vietnam war is making both sides compete in atrocity. We can presume, I believe, that the vast majority of Vietnamese in the North as well as the South would prefer peace under any regime to a continuation of the conflict.

My feelings about this war do not proceed from any anti-American bias. The sufferings, and also the moral degradation, to which the war exposes young conscripts from the United States, fill me with horror; and almost all my American friends share my hatred for the war.

On the other hand neither the moral nor the political issues at stake seem to me anything like so simple as they were in Spain. I cannot give the answers for which you ask without deciding what I think about a number of other questions. Is it our duty to prevent by force any seizure of a country by a foreign power? If we are wrong to support South Vietnam, what about the African countries, if they were attacked by neighboring white Governments? Were we right to connive at the seizure of West Irian by Indonesia, a Moslem power that despises most of the Papuans as idolaters? May not government by a foreign Communist power be the most hopeful means of bringing material progress to an impoverished country? Should we welcome a Chinese occupation of India? And (an even larger question) does industrialism usually bring more pleasure than pain to nonindustrial countries? These are all questions on which I have been unable to make up my mind.

Malcolm Muggeridge

First, I think the questions themselves oversimplify a very complex situation. The Spanish Civil War was itself complicated—more so than we knew at the time, *vide* Hugh Thomas's book—but not as complicated as the Vietnam situation. This is a manifestation of a cold war, in which the whole world, willy-nilly, is involved.

I hate the Cold War, as I do all wars; but I have to recognize that it exists, and that it can't by its nature be settled even by the total withdrawal or surrender of

one side. If, for instance, the Americans were to withdraw from Vietnam, the Cold War would then probably blow up in an active form in Siam or India, and the Americans would be faced with the same dilemma in those areas. If, on the other hand, the Communists were to abandon their efforts to pull Vietnam into the Chinese or Russian orbit, there would be one more artificial, American-supported country like South Korea, Formosa, etc., in the world.

Thus I cannot say that I am in favor of the intervention of the United States in Vietnam, any more than I am in favor of the intervention of the Chinese and Russians in Vietnam. But nor can I say that I am against the intervention of any of them because I recognize that, given the present state of affairs in the world, they consider that their intervention is an inescapable obligation. In other words, under no conceivable present circumstances will the South Vietnamese be left alone to arrange their own Government and way of life. Either they will have "communism" forced upon them or American-style "freedom"—both, I should suppose, abhorrent to the large majority of the population, as to the great majority of mankind.

This is the plight of the world in the middle of the twentieth century. It seems to me false and dangerously misleading to suggest that any particular aspect of this plight is capable of a solution on its own account, any more than, when I have a fever, it can be cured by cooling my hands or my feet.

It is easy to say that the Americans should get out of Vietnam, and equally easy to say that the Communists should be driven out of Vietnam. I say neither. I am deeply sorry for the suffering of the Vietnamese people, and deeply ashamed to live in a world whose ideologies can produce such suffering. I was equally ashamed of the Nazi and Stalinist concentration camps, and of the destruction of Dresden and Hiroshima. I hope that the world will recover from this sickness; but until it does, I will not comfort myself or others by pretending that the tragedy of Vietnam is due either to American or to Communist aggression, or that the withdrawal or surrender of one side or the other would end or even ameliorate the tragedy.

Lewis Mumford

The intervention of the United States in Vietnam is entirely without justification in either law, politics, or morals, and the progressive brutalization of American methods there has placed the United States Government in the infamous category of collective aggressors and exterminators. The crimes already committed by American forces under orders, from indiscriminate napalm bombing to crop poisoning and defoliation, equal the worst atrocities committed by Hitler, Stalin, and Mao. These practices betray the humane traditions of my country, expressed long ago by Emerson and Thoreau in their opposition to the Mexican War. No evils that totalitarian communism, in its most tyrannical form, might inflict upon Vietnam could possibly be worse than those already brought about by President Johnson's policy of ruthless aggression, which has fallen as heavily on the population that the United States was supposedly protecting as upon the people of North Vietnam. That policy is morally repulsive, politically bankrupt; and no military "victory" is possible.

This hideous situation is the outcome of the human delusions and pretensions brought about since 1945 by the exploitation of nuclear weapons and other forms of scientific genocide. It is a delusion to believe that the United States has the power, still less the authority, to police the world, as a self-appointed substitute for the United Nations. It is a delusion to believe that the powers of total destruction that both the United States and Soviet Russia—and perhaps, soon, China—possess can bring about security or peace or further any desirable constructive activity. It is a delusion to believe, as the present United States Government still does, that communism can be contained or destroyed by force of arms, though it is obvious that it is being modified and humanized by national interests and renewed national traditions, as well as by municipal, corporate, and regional interests that cannot be permanently suppressed by any system of totalitarian centralization, Communist or capitalist. Finally, it is a delusion to believe that any single economic system, political organization, or ideology is capable of dominating or controlling the great diversity of peoples and cultures throughout the planet, though by the continued growth of cooperative enterprises, under the aegis of the United Nations, a common culture may in time grow up that will humanize the purely mechanical modes of organization brought in by radio, television, jet planes, computers, and rockets. To achieve peace and comity the American people must cast aside these delusions of grandeur and power, and embrace the vital human realities that the belligerent Governments of our age have ignored, flouted, or deliberately sought to destroy.

What is the first step toward resolving the conflict in Vietnam? The first step is for the American Government to confess that its insidious intervention in the internal affairs of Vietnam was completely unjustified,

and the series of insidious commitments that have turned our supposed "democratic aid" into savage totalitarian aggression has been an unqualified political disaster and a moral disgrace. There is no honorable way out for the United States except to admit its errors and take whatever possible measures now are open to atone for the lives of the innocent civilians we have uprooted, massacred and tortured; to repair what we can of the damage we have done to soils and crops; and to dedicate our country to aid the people of Vietnam, North or South, whether "republican" or Communist. But the most pressing immediate duty, in order to overcome our massive political errors and military crimes, is the unconditional withdrawal of American forces from Vietnam, leaving the political rehabilitation of this country to the United Nations—insofar as any outside organization can be of any assistance in bringing peace and justice to the Vietnamese people.

Such an unconditional withdrawal would be an honest admission of the palpable reality; namely, that the insolent double-faced, demoralized policy the Johnson Administration has pursued has resulted in a humiliating defeat: not merely a moral defeat, which it has been from the beginning, but a military defeat which has exposed the impotence of mere destructive power to overcome the human spirit, when it is ready to sacrifice its home and life for the sake of its own ultimate integrity and continued existence. Such an admission of the military and political defeat of the United States, so far from being a confession of weakness, would be an assertion of the moral strength of the country, and of the reality of its vital traditions: the traditions of Washington and Jefferson, who, like the Vietnamese, opposed a far greater power; the traditions of Emerson and Thoreau, of Whitman and William James, who spoke most truly for their country when they spoke at the same time on behalf of the exploited, the oppressed, the enslaved, and the massacred.

Only if the people and the Congress of the United States recognize these realities and have the courage to act upon them will it be possible to keep the attack upon Vietnam from widening into an attack upon every person, group, or nation that dares to differ from the arrogant, self-righteous men who have foisted this war upon their own citizens and upon the Vietnamese.

Iris Murdoch

The American war in Vietnam is one of the more wantonly wicked political actions of the human race, appalling in its cold-bloodedness and alarming insofar as it is tolerated by a majority of persons in the moderately enlightened democratic country whose instrument of policy it is. From the technical point of view of international justice, since the Americans have no legitimate business in Vietnam and on their own admission prevented the holding of free elections since they objected to the Government which the Vietnamese people were likely freely to elect, the war is a war of unjustified aggression on the part of the USA. However, the callous will argue about technicalities. What is important is to stop being callous and to keep in mind that on every single day of this vicious war innocent people are being killed and maimed, and that the resources of modern technology are being deployed not to help but to shatter the tenuous civilization of a backward peasant country. Self-interest should check the Americans here. What is a military base compared with the hatred of half a continent? But plain morality also demands an end to a policy which causes such a mountain of suffering. If the American Government had any serious will to end this war, they could solve the problems involved in ending it. Or are they the slaves of the machine of evil which they have set up?

James Ngugi

I am totally against American intervention in Vietnam; against their use of gases and bombs to maintain a Fascist puppet regime; against their ruthless murder of a people whose only crime is their desire and determination to be free. How many times and for how long must fatherless children howl, widowed women cry, before imperialist intervention is finally exposed for what it is: tyranny masquerading under "democracy," "Free World," "the Great Society"?

So Johnson must be made to scram from Vietnam and from the whole of Southeast Asia. Why has he not used troops to impose democracy and freedom in the cities of Chicago and Los Angeles or in the Southern States? To give the American Negro at least such minimum rights as freedom from lynching, from wanton arrest, from hunger?

Hurrah for the National Liberation Front. Every blow they strike against the foe is a blow on behalf of the oppressed in Africa and everywhere else.

Edna O'Brien

I am against the intervention of the United States in Vietnam. I am against the intervention of all big nations in little nations (I am an Irishwoman) but I think the well-meaning, missionary attitude of the Americans is likely to do even more danger than that of the French, British, or Spanish who openly acknowledged that they were in another country to own, to exploit and to kill.

It is easy—too easy—to pronounce on what should be done in any corner of the world. I have never been to Vietnam, I do not understand the complexities of its people, its climate or its geography. Politically I would not know what is the ideal solution; but I do feel instinctively that the people of Vietnam, North and South, should be allowed to muddle their own way through, because that is the only true way. Outside intervention, like psychoanalysis in a person, is only a stopgap. It also seems ridiculous that we, in this country, a decadent society, should be thought wise or worthy enough to arbitrate on the fate of others.

C. Northcote Parkinson

In its foreign policy the United States is somewhat hampered by the US system of education in which ideology is strong and geography weak. A policy of containing communism everywhere may be theologically admirable but it is geographic nonsense. The United States cannot hold territory in Asia without appalling and useless bloodshed and expenditure. Strategically, the long-term purpose is and must be to prevent the Chinese occupying Australia. A war for this purpose would be fully justified, but no American in his senses should want, for this purpose, to give battle north of the Philippines and the Isthmus of Kra. And granted that such a conflict is inevitable (as it probably is) the time chosen is no more suitable than the battlefield. For the Chinese move southward has not even begun. The present American policy is thus to waste resources on a local conflict, forgetting that the main enemy is not in the field and may have no immediate plans relating to the area in dispute. It is possible to exhaust one's ammunition before the battle begins.

To draw attention to past mistakes is easier than to tell the President of the United States what he ought to do *now*. To disengage in 1966, after all that has taken place, would involve a great loss of prestige. This could best be minimized by bringing China into the United Nations, and indeed into the Security Council. The situation might then be internationalized and submitted to the UN Assembly. For the USA to accept a decision of the UN would be a moral gesture, less damaging than a military defeat. It is admittedly none too certain that the Chinese will now accept membership of the UN. Failing their acceptance, the only policy must be to make the best terms possible and withdraw in good order. Whatever face-saving may be devised, the effect would be one of defeat. The situation is already one of defeat, however, because the Americans are seeking peace and their local opponents are happy to continue the war. But defeat happens to all of us on occasion and refusal to accept defeat, on an ill-chosen battlefield, is often foolish. The better plan is to write off failure and reinforce success. And if anyone denies that there has been any success to reinforce he is quite obviously mistaken. Success has been considerable and it has happened exactly where it is wanted: in Indonesia.

Roger Peyrefitte

The United States has saved *my* civilization twice: freedom of thinking, of writing, of living. I am on their side everywhere throughout the world in their action for the defense of this civilization.

My entire solidarity with the United States in the Vietnam war does not lessen my sympathy, as a Frenchman, for North Vietnam, part of a land and of a nation which received the very ideas which led them to independence from my own country.

My solidarity with the United States doesn't make me approve of the war in itself as a means to resolve a conflict of ideologies, and I wish the promptest end of this one. I think the solution is in the hands of North Vietnam, by abandoning its propaganda, infiltration and conspiracies against South Vietnam, which make the war inevitable. Peace can be won only by the reciprocal respect of the rights of both sides.

It has already been proved in the same part of the world, by the results obtained in Korea, and in the rest of the world, by the pacific coexistence of two civilizations, that peace is always possible. In the same way, *our* countries show that people of different opinions can live together peacefully and sometimes amicably.

So, *vivent les États-Unis! et vive la paix!*

Harold Pinter

The Americans should not have gone in, but they did.
    They should now get out, but they won't.

William Plomer

1. Against it. I see it as a prolongation of one of the great mistakes of this century, America's backing of Chiang Kai-shek and blindness to the significance of Mao Tse-tung and the Chinese Revolution. I think it inconsistent with American generosity, to which we all owe much, and with American professions of democracy and Christianity. "Annihilation of life," said Tolstoy, "cannot be a means of the amelioration of life."

2. When I published my first book, my father said, "If you want to go to the Devil, you must go to the Devil in your own way." Let the Vietnamese go to the Devil in their own way. "Liberty begets anarchy," said Balzac, "anarchy leads to despotism, and despotism back to liberty. Millions have died without securing a triumph for any one system." Over to Tolstoy again: "No external conditions can guarantee our life, which is attended with inevitable sufferings and infallibly terminated by death, and which consequently can have no significance except in the constant accomplishment of what is demanded by the Power which has placed us in life with a sole certain guide—the rational conscience."

Anthony Powell

In 1937 I made mild fun (in the *Spectator*) of the published answers to Nancy Cunard's Spanish Civil War questionnaire. This pamphlet—on rereading—still seems to me to show writers at their silliest and most pompous, not to mention those anti-Fascist contributors who went to America or had to be conscripted, when it really came to "fighting Fascism" a couple of years later. Accordingly, I feel generally skeptical about the value of what T. S. Eliot called "collective activities on the part of men of letters"; more especially of two, so to speak, one-word answers to the complicated problem of Vietnam, as it were isolated from the political world situation.

J. B. Priestley

I have never been to Vietnam and write out of no special knowledge of the country, its people and problems. I imagine that most of the Vietnamese are simple and comparatively innocent people, who want to get on with their work and earn a little money, feed and raise their families, and enjoy some quiet nights. But this is what they are not able to do. They are trapped, so to speak, in an endless horror film. And this is not because they are at the mercy of appalling villains or sadistic madmen. It is because they are compelled to suffer for the illusions, blunders and follies of politicians and military men. They—the missing fathers, the screaming mothers, the shriveled and blinded babies—are the victims of a power struggle that is itself fundamentally idiotic. This is a strong statement and I propose to justify it. The Americans are fighting in Vietnam because they cling to the "domino" theory—that if all Vietnam goes Communist, then soon the whole of Southeast Asia will go Communist, and then before long all Asia will go Communist. But the men who believe this do not see communism as it actually is, a political-economic system that may be developed in many different ways and is always strongly influenced by nationalism. No, they see it as a vast monolithic conspiracy, a satanic plot to destroy all human liberty and happiness, an invasion of the earth from Hell. They are not thinking about the real world and real people at all.

It is this curious atmosphere of illusion and the lack of any real foundation that explain the daft policies and decisions of men who are not wicked and not necessarily quite stupid. (The Cold War, which led to the most extravagant and dangerous arms race the world has ever known, was itself based on an illusion.) They help to explain why, having decided to defeat the Vietcong, the American High Command proceeded to conduct its war in the worst possible way. Cunning and experienced guerrilla fighters, moving stealthily in the jungle, were to be defeated by bringing in millions of tons of explosive hardware, as if everybody was back in the Normandy Campaign. I am no military expert but I am sure that 75,000 troops, not put into combat until they had been carefully trained in guerrilla jungle warfare, might have achieved far more, certainly in the earlier stages, than these tons of hardware. And nothing, it seems, is learned from history. The Nazis were going to bomb us into submission in 1940. They didn't. We were going to defeat the German war effort by bombing in 1943–44. We didn't. But North Vietnam had to be bombed.

This is a war in which it is hard to distinguish combatants from noncombatants. Unless you are very careful or lucky, you kill or wound ten of the enemy and at the same time kill or wound fifty innocent civilians, with a high proportion of women and children among them. You also begin to destroy the very country you are supposed to be protecting. And surely one of the worst decisions ever arrived at by a command was that to make extensive use of napalm bombs. I am not thinking now in terms of a decent common humanity but simply considering this war as a series of decisions. Now one of its objects, perhaps its chief object, was to maintain or improve the prestige or "image" of America in world opinion. And the consequences of this napalm war have been disastrous. In my view, for what it is worth, more harm has been done to this prestige or "image," even among friendly peoples, than if the Americans had cleared out of Vietnam, two years ago, bag and baggage. All manner of aids and generosities have been forgotten in this glare of burning villages.

So much for bad decisions. But I shall be told that America has made promises and now has obligations in South Vietnam. True enough, but what the people want is to be left in peace, with a land still worth living in. Now here I may part company from some of my progressive friends, who are apt to imagine that life is like a Western with a cast of goodies and baddies. If the Americans are the baddies, then the Vietcong must be the goodies. But in my book they too seem to be ruthlessly pigheaded. They have murdered thousands and thousands of their fellow countrymen, and insist upon going on and on. Certainly they have not crossed the sea to drop napalm and high-explosive bombs and ruin the very land itself; but apparently they do have to go on and on. And I think it is time that they too, like the Americans, just stopped fighting.

I am no political expert—and sometimes I wish we hadn't so many of them, to keep the power struggle going—but this war is a huge senseless horror and instead of being "stepped up" by anybody, it ought to be stopped. Now if the Americans cannot sleep at night, haunted by the "domino" theory, let them cease fighting and retire to one fortified base for a year or two. If a sensible Government cannot be set up in South Vietnam for some time, then let the country be run temporarily by a UN commission, to get it going, steady it down, and at least prevent an orgy of vengeance. Let the North Vietnamese go home, and the Vietcong in the South put away their guns and start arguing instead of shooting. If they can persuade the other South Vietnamese that they would be better off under communism, then so be it—Vietnam becomes another Communist country. This won't keep me awake at night, even though I happen to believe that communism is a clumsy and expensive system that will inevitably have to be modified. (Just as inevitable developments, such as automation, will compel America to adopt some socialist measures.) What does keep me awake at night is the thought of this daft horrible war, which only needs more blind escalation to drive us all to the edge of Doomsday.

D. N. Pritt

I am opposed to the United States intervention in Vietnam, not merely on grounds of humanity, but because this intervention is a breach of international law, and in particular of the Charter of the United Nations.

In international law, it is surely clear that the United States, a country lying many thousands of miles from Vietnam, and not attacked or threatened by Vietnam, has *prima facie* no right to be waging war in that country, and the question whether its intervention can be justified may therefore fairly be approached from the angle that the burden lies on the United States and those who support it to justify its intervention.

Before I study the arguments that have been and are being advanced to discharge that burden, it is useful to examine the Geneva Agreements of 1954, which provide the background of the problem. Up to 1954, Vietnam was, and had long been, one undivided country, often occupied by foreign powers but never wholly subdued; and the Geneva negotiations and Agreements followed on a decisive military defeat inflicted by the Vietnamese people on the French occupants. The primary object of the negotiations and Agreements was to secure the future of Vietnam as one sovereign independent state. There was a secondary object; since part of Vietnam—a portion of what is now called South Vietnam—was still occupied by the French, it was necessary to provide not only for the future government of Vietnam but also for its interim administration during the period—expected to be about two years—required for clearing up the aftermath of a long war and establishing an independent sovereign Vietnam.

The Agreements provided that the future form of government should be determined by a general election "which will bring about the re-unification of Vietnam," to be held in July 1956; and they provided that the control and administration of territory north of the 17th parallel in the interim period should be entrusted to the Democratic Republic of Vietnam, which had been established in 1945, immediately after the expulsion of the Japanese, as the Government of Vietnam, while the control and administration of the territory to the south should be entrusted to the French. (The French had established a rather shadowy "State of Vietnam," with one Bao Dai, a former puppet king of Annam, who lived on the French Riviera, as Emperor. This shadowy

state was represented at the Geneva negotiations, but no one treated it seriously enough to demand that it be made a party to the Agreements.) It is important to realize how the Agreements treated the 17th parallel; they declared it to be a "military demarcation line," and to be "provisional and . . . not in any way [to] be interpreted as constituting a political or territorial boundary."

The importance of the Agreements, and their validity and operation, were scarcely affected by the fact that the United States did not sign them, not because the United States was not important, but because it committed itself to observe them as fully as if it had actually signed; by a formal Declaration made at the time of the signature, it not merely "took note" of them but undertook to refrain from the threat or use of force to disturb them, in accordance with Article 2 of the Charter of the United Nations (which lays down that "all Members shall refrain in their international relations from the threat or use of force against the territorial integrity or political independence of any state, or in any other manner inconsistent with the Purposes of the United Nations").

The United States went further in this Declaration; it added that it would "continue to seek to achieve unity through free elections supervised by the United Nations to insure that they are conducted fairly"; and it reiterated "its traditional position that peoples are entitled to determine their own future and that it will not join in an arrangement which will hinder this."

It is thus clear that there was then no question of any permanent division of Vietnam into two states, and the frequent assertions of American politicians—in particular that of President Johnson on August 12, 1964—that the Agreements "guaranteed the independence of *South* Vietnam" were and are the exact opposite of the truth.

With that background, I can now turn to study the arguments put forward by or on behalf of the United States to justify its intervention in the teeth of Article 2 of the United Nations Charter quoted above. Most of these arguments are founded on one or another of the exceptions to the general rule of Article 2 which can be found in other Articles.

The first argument rests on Article 51, which preserves "the inherent right of individual or collective self-defense if an armed attack occurs against *a Member of the United Nations.*"

Can it be said that the United States intervened in Vietnam under the right of individual or collective self-defense? So far as individual self-defense goes, the United States had not been attacked; and if one thinks of individual self-defense for South Vietnam, the insuperable difficulty is that that entity—whatever its precise status—is not a member of the United Nations. As for collective self-defense, this can be invoked only for members of regional collective systems, and the United States is not in any Southeast Asian region.[1]

The only other exception to the prohibition of Article 2 is to be found in Article 53; this Article gives the American case no help, since the actions which it permits cannot be carried out by any state or regional agency without the authorization of the Security Council, which has not been given.

There is one other Article in the United Nations Charter which ought to be noticed; this is Article 39, which gives the United Nations Organization the right to intervene in civil strife whenever that threatens international peace; but this right rests in the United Nations alone, and cannot be used by states.

Thus, all arguments based directly on Articles of the Charter are of no use to the United States' case; but there is another argument, plausible and frequently invoked, to the effect that:

(1) South Vietnam is a sovereign state, and the present hostilities—to the extent to which North Vietnam is engaged in them—are a war between two states, and are therefore not civil strife.[2]

(2) Since it is a sovereign state, South Vietnam may lawfully ask the United States to help it in the war, to resist aggression from North Vietnam, and the United States may lawfully act on that request.[3]

[1] If it be asserted that the existence of the Southeast Asia Treaty Organization, which consists mainly of countries outside Southeast Asia, creates some right in the United States to intervene, the answer is that the Southeast Asia Treaty is expressed not to "affect . . . in any way the rights and obligations of any of the Parties under the Charter of the United Nations."

[2] The argument leads to odd conclusions, for all the fighting—as distinct from the bombing of North Vietnam by US forces—has taken and is taking place in South Vietnam, between two groups of inhabitants of South Vietnam, the one helped often enough by the United States and the other by troops from North Vietnam; and it is not easy to imagine hostilities which are at one and the same time a civil war in one country and a war between two states!

[3] The assertion that North Vietnam has been guilty of aggression against South Vietnam is baseless. It is not merely that—as we have already seen—at the most what North Vietnam is doing is to take part in a civil war in Vietnam, but it is clear that the cause of the fighting, and of the endless crises, in South Vietnam was not any aggression from the North, but the unpopularity of the puppet governments and of the United States. Civil war in South Vietnam began at least as early as 1957, and no evidence has been produced of any participation of North Vietnam in hostilities in South Vietnam earlier than 1960.

This argument in its turn can be convincingly answered:

(1) It is really impossible in international law to recognize South Vietnam and its Government as sovereign. The well-known requirements for such recognition are that the Government is supported by the majority of the people, and that it exercises *de facto* control over the territory which it claims to govern; but the facts are that at every stage of its history that we need to consider the purported Government of "South Vietnam" in the saddle at the moment has never been supported by more than about one third of the people, nor has it controlled more than about one third of the territory. There is no doubt that the present Government of South Vietnam, like the many that have preceded it, would disappear in a day or two if the United States withdrew support from it.

(2) Even if it could be made out that South Vietnam and its Government could be regarded as sovereign, the United States would still have no justification for intervention, for Article 2 of the Charter still binds it not to take part in war unless it can bring itself within Article 51 or any other Article of that nature; and this, as we have seen, it cannot do. The infiltration of North Vietnamese troops into the long-established civil war in South Vietnam could not possibly be regarded as armed attack on a member of the United Nations within the carefully drawn terms of Article 51. The truth is that the days of "world gendarmes" are gone, and the notion that the request or consent of the "Government" of South Vietnam, which is wholly dependent on the United States and would make any request and give any consent that the United States wanted, can create a right in the United States to take part in the war is not even plausible.

It should not be overlooked that in any case the United States can scarcely justify its intervention in the war, in which its express object is to keep South Vietnam separate from the North, when it pledged itself at Geneva to seek to achieve the *unity* of Vietnam, and not to join in any arrangements which would hinder the determination of the Vietnamese people—the people of the whole of Vietnam—of their future.

I should add, since there is such incessant talk of aggression by North Vietnam, that it is really meaningless to suggest that the participation by the Government of one half of a country, expressly declared by international agreements to be one country, in a civil war raging in the other half can constitute aggression by one state against another.

I have now, I think, answered every assertion worthy of the name of argument that has been advanced to justify United States intervention in Vietnam, and need only deal briefly with statements, not worthy of being regarded as arguments, which are frequently made, to the effect that the United States is intervening to "protect freedom" and to "contain communism." Such statements have no substance, of course, in international law, but they are worth a few observations, because, however false in essence, they do go near to disclosure of the real motives of the United States Government, which are to prevent at all costs, however terrible, any extension whatever, in any part of the world, of Communist prestige or influence. It was with this object that, from the moment of the conclusion of the Geneva Agreements, the fanatically anti-Communist John Foster Dulles introduced and supported the fanatically anti-Communist Ngo Dinh Diem first as Prime Minister and then as President of "South Vietnam," and encouraged him to refuse throughout 1954–56 and indeed later to take any part in the preparation, let alone the holding, of the elections provided for by the Geneva Agreements. The real reason for refusal was that both the United States and Diem feared—rightly enough—that the elections would result in victory for the principles of the Democratic Republic of Vietnam under Ho Chi Minh, and were determined to avoid this; the pretext advanced was that any elections in which Communist North Vietnam took part would not be "free," a pretext particularly baseless in view of the fact that such elections had been agreed on at Geneva and that Article 7 of the Final Declaration at Geneva had been deliberately worded to invalidate any such pretext.

When I come to the question how the conflict should be resolved, it is clear from what I have written above and from Articles 16 to 18 of the Geneva Agreements [4] that United States forces, material, and bases have no right to be present in Vietnam, and ought to be withdrawn. Since the United States has indicated—see, e.g., *The New York Times* of January 2, 1966—its acceptance of the Geneva Agreements as a basis for peace negotiations, and has thus plainly accepted in principle that its troops, etc., should be withdrawn, it is logically inevitable that they should be withdrawn without delay. Peace negotiations must always go by stages, and in my view the most practical steps are that:

(1) all United States attacks on North Vietnam should be halted at once;

[4] Article 16: "the introduction into Vietnam of any troop reinforcements and additional military personnel is prohibited";

Article 17: "the introduction into Vietnam of any reinforcements in the form of all [*sic*] types of arms, munitions and other war material . . . is prohibited";

Article 18: "the establishment of new military bases is prohibited throughout Vietnam territory."

(2) negotiations for cessation of hostilities and ultimate peace terms should start on the footing that the National Liberation Front of South Vietnam should take part therein as one of the belligerents, and that the Geneva Agreements be accepted as governing;

(3) the introduction of United States and of other foreign troops associated with them, and of material, into Vietnam should cease immediately;

(4) the withdrawal of United States' troops and material, and those of other foreign countries associated with them, should begin at once, and the "phasing" of further withdrawals should be agreed in the negotiations.

James Purdy

I am opposed to intervention by the United States of America in Vietnam, but such mass massacres seem to me inescapable as long as the content of the American mind is cigarette and liquor ads, its religion dope-sex, its people millionaire movie and baseball stars. Vietnam is atrocious for the dead and maimed innocent, but it's probably sadder to be a live American with only the Madison Avenue gibbers for a homeland and a God.

Kathleen Raine

You ask me as a poet questions which I cannot, as a poet, answer. Politics, and war, are not the weapons of poets; though both may at times have to be used in the defense of Civilization. I follow Churchill in believing that civilization may sink if we cease to be willing to defend it, with life if necessary; and it seems to have fallen to America, at this time, to defend a way of life which at least makes possible civilized values, and human freedom, against the advance of communism.

I cannot possibly form a judgment of all the issues involved in the Vietnam war. It seems on the face of it that (as in Cyprus) the Vietnamese have very little to gain by the battle being fought on their land; on the other hand I think America must hold the frontiers against communism, and Vietnam is at present the scene of a conflict which might become a great deal worse if America were to withdraw. Recent developments in China may well remind us of the gravity of the threat. I wish that General de Gaulle, the only great statesman left in the world, had the handling of it; both his master-touch and sense of what is possible seem to be wanting in the present American Administration.

But Caesar's world is really not the kingdom which concerns me and I am unqualified to pronounce upon it.

Frederic Raphael

I answer these questions with reluctance. I am not among those who imagine that my word should be law. On the other hand, of course, I am opposed to the quantity if not necesarily to the whole idea of American intervention in Vietnam. (It does not seem to me that there is anything necessarily wicked in giving aid to one's friends, though one may doubt the wisdom of other people's choice of friends.) However, I have little doubt that the Americans have been led into an indefensible position.

The atrocious weapons which they are using and their cynical support of an absurd and brutal puppet are nothing but repugnant, yet the brutalities of the Vietcong can be ignored only by those who delight in doctrinaire blindness. Ultimately, however, the mutilations and killings are so appalling and so blatantly disproportionate to the importance of any "favorable" solution that it is disgusting, even if it is in a certain light understandable, to lend them support. How can one agree to the destruction of an entire country in order to save a few houses from possible dry rot? Where does one draw the line? *Somewhere*—and somewhere before the present situation.

Withdrawal might be much uglier than some simplists pretend. Comparison with the Spanish Civil War (where support of the Government would have been mandatory for any believer in democracy) seems to me tendentious. The notion of legality versus illegality scarcely has sense in a world in which semantic manipulation has become an applauded form of sponsored prostitution (public relations). In the end the only reasonable comparison is with Algeria, from which even the King of the Ostriches was obliged to withdraw.

Simon Raven

1. Since England has abdicated from Empire yet failed to align herself with Europe, she has become a client kingdom of America. It is a rash client who opposes the policies of a munificent protector.

2. I was once taught, as a young professional soldier, that military failure must never be reinforced. I was also taught that it must never be confessed.

Herbert Read

The presence of the forces of the United States in Vietnam cannot be defended on any ground other than that of political expediency, and such expediency is based on an almost infantile conception of social realities. Nearly every American one meets—even those who question or oppose the invasion of Southeast Asia—is obsessed by something he calls "the Communist menace." But as anyone knows who has visited China or India, or is familiar with the social and economic conditions in that part of the world, what is called communism, for more than ninety per cent of the people, is a simple faith in the future, a determination to recover national independence and self-respect, to reconstitute a civilization that for centuries has been torn by internal dissensions and corrupted by foreign exploitation. This resurgence is now so strong in China and Southeast Asia that no power on earth will ever destroy it. Like all faiths, it has its dogmas and inquisitions, but it is the will of the people, opposed only by a minority of ex-landlords and ex-capitalists. To support these minorities in the name of freedom or democracy is the utmost cant or hypocrisy.

The only possibility of stemming this tide of self-determination and national pride in Asia is to lay waste vast territories by the brutal and inhuman application of the terrible weapons of destruction possessed by the United States. To go to this extreme would certainly lead to a Third World War and the end of our civilization. That the people of the United States, through their elected representatives, can be so blind and misled is beyond reasonable belief, but the process of "escalation" goes on inexorably, and only the conscience of the whole of the uncommitted world can now halt it. But conscience must be more than a state of moral outrage: it must be active. The United States must be ostracized in every international organization. Support for all its external policies must be withheld. We must not repeat the mistakes of the years 1936–39, when indifference and pharisaic neutrality were the determining causes of a world war. With every force at our disposal, personal and national, we must oppose the rulers of the United States until they admit their false reasoning and obsessional fears, and withdraw unconditionally from the inferno of hatred and destruction which they have willfully created.

Mary Renault

I am a historical novelist. Experience at this job makes me doubt the usefulness of making snap judgments on complex human situations of which one knows, by serious standards of evidence, nothing whatever. Where I do know something, I find such facility impossible.

I can recognize only two qualifications for offering advice about the Vietnam war, or any other foreign affairs: personal knowledge of the place, or special inside information. Lacking these, it does not seem to me that writers, merely by reason of their trade, are any better placed in this regard than doctors, engineers, or indeed any other men and women literate enough to read the newspapers and weeklies.

The moral concern of writers should be with the effect of their own works upon their readers. This is a matter within their own control, for which they have the sole responsibility.

Kenneth Rexroth

1. I am against it.
2. It should stop.

David Riesman

I was in Japan in the fall of 1961. This was the time when General Maxwell Taylor, Walt Rostow, and Joseph Alsop went to Vietnam in a highly publicized mission to look the situation over. I could share the shudder which went through the deeply sensitive Japanese intellectual community at that time and the fear that, if the United States became more heavily embroiled in Vietnam, the position of Japan, caught between the United States and mainland China, would almost necessarily become more precarious. I, myself, felt no less anxious; and since that time, although I have not followed events in Southeast Asia at all closely and have no familiarity with the area, Vietnam has been a sort of recurring nightmare for me—and one which I share not only with many Americans but also with many Japanese friends who continue to write me agitated letters, the more so if they are sympathetic with the best in the American tradition and hate to see the tradition debased and exploited by the use of such terms as freedom and democracy to hide the actual brutality and stupidity which so largely characterize our presence in that country.

I say this although I realize that there are idealists both in this country and in South Vietnam who see the war there, as perhaps Walt Rostow himself does, in terms of stages of economic and social development in a more humane direction. Among some of the military and some of the AID and civilian groups we have sent to Vietnam, there are dedicated missionaries who want to help that country. They believe, and are quite possibly correct in this, that the Vietcong under North Vietnamese domination would if victorious impose a regime of thought reform on the country on a Chinese model. They do not see the war, as so many Americans do, as a pawn in a comic-strip showdown with world communism, or a counter in domestic American politics (for example vis-à-vis Republican charges that the Democrats "lost" China), or as a test of national will on the world scene. I suppose in a paradoxical way I am more nationalistic than they are, more fearful of the damage this war is doing to American society than hopeful about or generous toward any possible benefits of even a combined military and civilian missionary enterprise in Vietnam.

I have never been defeatist about American power in the world: the power of example and imitation. I think we would be far stronger and more influential if we were less militaristic and in that sense less defensive. Unlike some of my friends, I do not regard the war in Vietnam as an inevitable outcome of imperialistic or racist or even hysterical attitudes within the United States, although of course it draws sustenance from all of these. The excision of this cancer at an earlier stage—in many earlier stages—seems to me quite conceivable: Consider in this connection President Eisenhower's veto of the hope of Admiral Radford and Vice President Nixon that we come to the aid of the French and bomb Dien Bien Phu in 1954. The war draws strength from many forces which are in principle controllable, such as interservice rivalry or the still unappeased vindictiveness of the Pacific-minded generals and politicians vis-à-vis the Atlantic-minded ones. We do lack a Republican general who can come in and make peace.

While international pressures may conceivably force both sides to negotiation, I do not see any political force within America strong enough to reverse our course other than the President himself. In this situation I am willing to work for what may seem to some of those opposed to our Government's policy to be relatively small advances. I do consider it an advance to work in every way toward de-escalation, reducing the cruelty and savagery of the war, the harm done to the target populations and indirectly to ourselves. That is why the enclave view recently propounded by General Gavin and George Kennan has seemed to me a platform which could acquire sizable support and which could be introduced *de facto* as the same sort of tacit arms control we have sometimes reached with the Soviet Union. Not being a complete pacifist but only a ground-army pacifist, I would consider this a very large gain. To see on television explosions of bombs day after day, and score kept of the Vietcong—or supposedly Vietcong—dead, seems to me gruesome fodder for the American imagination. I am old-fashioned enough to feel that there is something inherently indecent about the bombing of civilian populations, and perhaps too despairing in not imagining that I will be able to live in a world in my lifetime in which all violence is outlawed. But such a world is indeed conceivable to me eventually, if we can moderate the grossest violence while the concept of the unity of mankind takes slow and painful root among us.

Alain Robbe-Grillet *

Against all military intervention in Vietnam, certainly, and against all war in general, since it settles nothing.

Harold Rosenberg

I am opposed to the character which the intervention has assumed. No argument yet given in support of the US military campaign justifies the pursuit of native people by teams of well-fed foreigners thoroughly trained and equipped with the most advanced scientific means for putting them to death. This is what is actually happening as revealed to us daily in pictures and words that defile every principle of fair play taught us from childhood. We can escape the shame of these images only through ruining our sense of fact and corrupting our language. This is Washington's present contribution to American culture.

The conflict can be ended with the United States guaranteeing the protection of persons of South Vietnam who reject communism. It cannot be ended if the real aim of the United States is to be the boss of Asia.

Philip Roth

The following article, describing the final solution of the Bensuc problem, appeared on page 4 of *The New York Times,* January 11, 1967:

BENSUC, South Vietnam, Jan. 8—For years this quiet, ill-kept village hugging an elbow of the Saigon River 30 miles northwest of the capital has been a haven for the Vietcong. One pacification program after another has failed here and since a Government military post was abandoned more than a year ago, Bensuc has been considered a "hostile" village. It has been an embarrassing problem for Saigon.

This morning 600 allied soldiers—mostly Americans—descended on the village and began "solving" the problem. Within two weeks the more than 3,800 residents of Bensuc will be living in a new refugee settlement 20 miles to the southeast and it is likely that the tattered huts and small shops here will be flattened by bulldozers. The village of Bensuc, which for so long served as a meeting place for Vietcong political cadres and as a supply point for insurgent troops in two provinces, will be swept from the face of the earth. "This is probably the only military or political solution for this place," said an American colonel.

Allied officers in Bensuc acknowledged that the residents might be reluctant to leave their property and the revered graves of their ancestors, but they said that new land would be given to them along with frame, tin-roofed homes that will be "a lot better than what they have now." Vietcong villages are typically found in disrepair, but Bensuc is an extreme example. There is no evidence that any new buildings have been put up in months. The old ones are crumbling and chronic illness is widespread. Firmly supporting the resettlement, the colonel said: "I imagine there will be a lot of wailing and gnashing of teeth, but they'll do what they're told."

Sixty helicopters landed the troops in seven clearings within the village walls this morning so a human net could be quickly drawn around the residents and the soldiers could avoid the maze of booby traps around Bensuc. Shortly afterward, a helicopter equipped with loudspeakers began broadcasting this message: "Attention people of Bensuc! You are surrounded by Republic of South Vietnam and allied forces. Do not run away or you will be shot as V.C. Stay in your homes and wait for further instructions from the air and on the ground. You will not be hurt if you follow instructions." Then came a second message telling men, women and children: "Go immediately to the schoolhouse. Anyone who does not go to the schoolhouse will be considered a V.C. and treated accordingly."

Most of the residents, considered to be passive Vietcong, followed the instructions. Forty-one did not and during the day they were tracked down and killed. There was little question that the men fleeing on bicycles, crawling through rice paddies and thrashing in the murky river were Vietcong. Some carried rifles, others wore packs. Three were discovered at the mouth of a cave with an assortment of surgical instruments and commercially produced drugs. At the schoolhouse the people were separated into groups according to age and sex, interrogated, given a warm meal and were seen by an army doctor. One hundred males 15 to 45 years old, unable to prove their identity, were taken away as Vietcong suspects. Eleven men were judged on the spot to be Vietcong.

The villagers were allowed to file home this evening, but tomorrow they will be ordered back to the school, their homes will be searched and in a day or so more the troops will begin loading them into barges for the trip downstream. Part of their houses, their furniture and their livestock will go with them. "It takes time and it's troublesome, but I think you find a little less resentment if you take everything they've got and move it with them," said Brig. Gen. James F. Hollingworth, an assistant commander of the United States First Infantry Division.

The move into the village was the opening part of an allied operation called Cedar Falls. More than 15,000 soldiers are being deployed in what the military describes as the most thorough search ever of the 60 square miles of the Thanhdien Forest and the thick jungle that the Americans call the Iron Triangle. Intelligence officers believe there may be no more than 100 enemy soldiers in the 60 square miles. But they hope to find a tunnel the length of the seven-mile-long triangle and to disrupt operations at the headquarters of Vietcong Military Region 4. The headquarters, which controls Vietcong operations in and around Saigon, has been traced to the triangle.

The allied goal at Bensuc was to deny the Vietcong a strategic base and to capture important political figures. At least three of the eleven taken today appear to be prime suspects. The Allies also believe that they will be able to win the allegiance of the people once they have been removed from the Vietcong sphere.
The Allies also believe that they will be able to win the

allegiance of the people once they have been removed from the Vietcong sphere. After leveling their homes, their shops, and the graves of their ancestors with a bulldozer. Who can be "for" such a war as we are fighting?

Richard H. Rovere

I regard our military presence in Vietnam as mistaken and dangerous. I do not share all the moral outrage expressed by certain other American writers. I agree with Arthur Schlesinger, Jr., that what we are witnessing is a tragedy without villains. I oppose our intervention because of its scale and its futility—and because of the damage it is doing to institutions I value.

I must say that I think that opposition to intervention raises certain questions that have yet to be examined by most people who favor withdrawal. Like Senator Fulbright, I think that foreign aid can be a road to war and that our involvement in Vietnam came about in large part as a consequence of the nonmilitary aid we gave to the South Vietnamese Government in the middle and late fifties. We acquired an interest in the survival not only of the state but of the regime in charge. This could happen anywhere, and I think we must reexamine our whole policy toward underdeveloped countries in the light of what has happened in Vietnam. To my mind, we should seriously consider abandoning unilateral aid in favor of aid administered by the UN or some other international agency.

I think we should now stop all bombing, North and South, and all military activity except the defense of those areas in which the Government of South Vietnam is in firm control. Within those areas we can offer sanctuary to all who desire it. The rest, it seems to me, must be up to the Government of South Vietnam. If it wishes to pursue the war, that is its business. No doubt General Ky would claim a betrayal by us. But General Ky is not irreplaceable. And later this year, if the military junta allows it to happen, there will be a civilian Government that should determine its own foreign policy. If General Ky blocks the formation of that Government, then we should have nothing further to do with his junta. If a civilian Government is in power, we should negotiate with it a treaty providing for our continued presence on very limited terms and for a limited period of time.

Bertrand Russell

The war in Vietnam is one of brutal aggression, as despicable and wrong a war as any I can recall. So often people who profess to be concerned about social justice and world peace treat conflict as an unfortunate occurrence in which each side deserves equal blame for disturbing comfortable people in the West.

What is at stake in Vietnam was set out as clearly as could be wished by President Eisenhower in 1953:

> Now let us assume we lost Indochina. If Indochina goes, the tin and tungsten we so greatly value would cease coming. We are after the cheapest way to prevent the occurrence of something terrible—the loss of our ability to get what we want from the riches of the Indochinese territory and from Southeast Asia.

The United States, which controls sixty per cent of the world's natural resources, is waging a war of aggression—an imperialist war such as that fought by the Japanese in Southeast Asia. In the South 59 per cent of the rural population were put in barbed wire camps under conditions of forced labor. It is not sufficiently appreciated that more Vietnamese died between 1954 and 1960 than since 1960 when the National Liberation Front began its popular resistance on the model of the Yugoslav partisans and the French Maquis. Because the US Government is preparing to suppress national uprisings against US domination the world over, barbarous experimentation has been the salient feature of the American assault on Vietnam. Poison gas and chemicals, phosphorus and napalm, the systematic bombardment of hospitals, schools, sanatoria and leprosaria have gone on, virtually without our serious concern in the West, year after year.

I regard the policy makers in Washington who preside over both the aggression and the atrocity to be war criminals in the precise sense laid down at the Nuremberg trials. The obligation upon every decent human being is to support the Vietnamese—to regard them as we did the Jews of the Warsaw Ghetto in relation to the Gestapo. The issue is as stark and the necessity for an American defeat and withdrawal as paramount. We *must* understand that the torment of Vietnam, like that of Spain in the 1930's, is a barbarous rehearsal.

William Sansom

With no firsthand knowledge, no access to underclared political motives, and what is most important, without reliable information on who has done what about a conference, the question becomes one not of judgment but of emotions, of horror and pity and disgust. Otherwise . . . Munich, we think—therefore no withdrawal. Then we see that escalation looks even more dangerous —therefore retreat. It is a war between man plus vegetation and man plus machines which seems to have no military solution, and in which the fury of technological pride can rage as persistently as any ideological fervor.

However, impasses have been overcome before: new minds, new thinking come along. Loss of face does not matter so much—Russia did not lose much over Cuba, nor France over Algeria. The final importance of face is to behave so that you can look yourself in yours— difficult at a time when acceptance of the idea of torture is almost casual. But even so, to give an opinion, from the outside, without exact evidence, is useless. It is not as though a withdrawal means the end of pain and killing: if that were so, the choice would be plain.

Nathalie Sarraute *

I think that the conflict in Vietnam stems from a popular revolt against an oppressive regime. The American intervention which, having provoked that of North Vietnam, has led to "escalation," is consequently quite unjustified.

The only possible solution of the conflict therefore seems to me to be the suspension of bombing, followed by the withdrawal of American and North Vietnamese forces, accompanied by neutralization of the whole of Vietnam.

Arthur M. Schlesinger, Jr.

It seems to me meaningless to ask whether one is "for" or "against" the American intervention in Vietnam. That intervention, for better or for worse, is a fact. The real question today is whether one is "for" the immediate termination of that intervention or "for" its continuation until a negotiated settlement can be achieved.

On this question, I am for a negotiated settlement. The object of such a settlement should be, in my judgment, the neutralization under UN supervision of all four states created by the Geneva Accords of 1954 (Laos, Cambodia, North and South Vietnam).

Obviously the Vietcong and Hanoi will not negotiate so long as they think they are going to win. Since a military stalemate is the self-evident and indispensable precondition to negotiation, the continued presence of American troops is plainly necessary.

Nor, in my view, will the Vietcong and Hanoi negotiate so long as they feel that the United States is out to destroy them and that their very survival is at stake. I am therefore opposed to the widening of the war and believe that bombing should be tapered off in the North and used very sparingly in the South. There is no point in trying to save a country by obliterating it. I also believe that the Vietcong should be included in the negotiations and that the prospect should be held out to them of a say in the future political life of South Vietnam, conditioned on their laying down their arms, opening up their territories and abiding by the ground rules of a free election. I do not think that a negotiated solution along these or any lines will be easy to get. I do not have the impression that either side has tried hard enough to get one.

I am opposed to an immediate American withdrawal (a) because it would end all possibility of a negotiated settlement, (b) because it would deliver the people of Vietnam to the Vietcong, who would undoubtedly jail and murder a good many, especially among the students and intellectuals, and condemn the rest to a bleak Communist despotism, (c) because of the effect it would have in neighboring countries, especially on the gallant struggle of the Laotian neutralists under Prince Souvanna Phouma to maintain their independence. Also I find something distasteful about those sitting in ease in Europe and America who would righteously hand over a country to a tough Communist crew on the ground, evidently, that, though they wouldn't much like communism for themselves, it will be just great for the Vietnamese.

As for the question whether, if we were starting all over again, one would favor this kind of American entanglement in Vietnam, the answer is obviously no. As George Kennan said, "If we were not already involved as we are today, I know of no reason why we should wish to become so involved." Very few people, even in the Pentagon, would have freely and deliberately chosen to land the United States in this particular quagmire. But this is a question of interest to those who deal with the past rather than the present—to historians rather than to statesmen. Given the forbidding situation we face today, I am in favor of trying for a negotiated solution.

Ramón Sender *

My first and foremost thought is rather discouraging. It seems very likely that the war in Vietnam may be the prologue to a third world war, as the Spanish Civil War was a prologue to the Second.

I should be delighted to be proved wrong, but all the signs point in that direction. The third war would begin with mutual promises and prohibitions over the use of nuclear weapons, but naturally they will be used by whichever nation sees itself in imminent danger of being defeated.

In short, the war in Vietnam is the prologue to an atomic war which at the moment seems disastrously inevitable.

The most extraordinary thing is that it will not be a question of war between the capitalist and the socialist worlds. Capitalism today is not the same as in Marx's day, nor have the regimes of Moscow and Peking anything to do with the socialism of Marx and Bakunin. An atomic war, if it does occur, will be between two tendencies which are working in the same direction: revolution through abundance (USA) and revolution through hopelessness and misery (China).

Irwin Shaw

This book has had an ominous predecessor. In the 1930's a representative selection of writers were asked to state their views on the Spanish Civil War and their opinions were published. As I remember it, well over a hundred of the writers declared themselves on the side of the Loyalists and condemned Franco and his German and Italian allies. One writer, I believe, opted for Franco, and two were neutral. In 1939, the war was over, Franco had won, and World War II was a few months in the offing.

Without seeing any of the results of the present survey, I am willing to predict that the great majority of the writers questioned will deplore the intervention of the United States in Vietnam. It will thus be demonstrated that writers are in general more humane and gifted with greater political acumen than most senators; we will be pleased with ourselves and our combined opinions will have no effect on the outcome of the war.

Unlike many of our commentators and officeholders and military leaders, I have no theory about how we could win the war in Vietnam immediately. But I do know how President Johnson, who is worried that the opinion of the American people on the subject of the war is divided, could rally all Americans to his side.

All the President would have to do is lend the North Vietnamese three or four of our aircraft carriers and let them sail back and forth off Cape Cod, without any danger of being attacked, while sending off waves of bombers to shower Boston, New York, Philadelphia and the suburbs in between with high-explosive, napalm and defoliating chemicals for a year or two. The bombing should be planned in such a way that a great number of the casualties would be sustained by children. At the same time millions of pamphlets should be dropped stating that all this was being done for us in the holy name of peace and religion, the religion in this case being international communism. A good proportion of the children should come from families who out of a secret admiration for communism or a sick desire for tranquillity had conspired to help the invaders. After two or three casualties in each family, the parents, along with all other Americans, would be convinced that the United States would have to win the war at any cost, even if it meant fighting to the last man and continuing hostilities for a century.

Konstantin Simonov *

I am unconditionally against US armed intervention in Vietnam, whatever the reasons with which they endeavor to justify it.

To resolve the conflict I think that, to begin with, it is necessary to return to the Geneva Convention and fulfill its clauses honestly and completely. If this is done as the first and absolutely essential step, then in the future all the remaining unsettled problems will at least not be resolved under the hail of bombs nor in an atmosphere of murder.

In addition to all this, I feel that the measure of suffering of the Vietnamese nation exceeded the limits long ago. Mankind does not have the moral right to allow this to continue. In using the word "mankind," I realize how deep differences of political opinion among the various representatives of this mankind can go; nevertheless this is precisely the word that I wish to use.

C. P. Snow

I have always thought—and I have said so in the United States years ago—that the American intervention in Vietnam was wrong. For many reasons: among them, and to me the most compelling, that in modern conditions a technologically advanced country fighting a primitive one is going to be at a hopeless moral disadvantage. The advanced country, as I said in Parliament in July, will use—and has used—weapons of indiscriminate homicide. Inevitably it will kill—and has killed—more innocent persons than the primitive country can touch. It is possible, by the ultimate use of this process, that America can devastate the whole of Vietnam, North and South, and so, in the short term, "win" the war. But the price will affect the whole Western world for generations.

The first necessary step is to stop the strategic bombing of North Vietnam. Once this is done, the forces of reason, both in the Western world and in the Soviet Union, stand a finite chance.

Edgar Snow

For the United States intervention? Could any rational American seriously be *for* a Chinese armed occupation of Canada or Mexico undertaken in violation of the United Nations Charter and of international treaties, in order to organize and finance pro-Communist, anti-American, and pro-Chinese dictatorship over our neighbors—by means of a war of bombs and napalm hurled from the air to burn and destroy the habitations, the fields, the forests, and all the works as well as many of the lives of men, women and children who never harmed China? No, I am not *for* the United States armed occupation of Vietnam, which is the equivalent of the above hypothesis.

The conflict can be resolved by the United States abandoning politically fruitless attempts to decide, unilaterally, and by nationalistic law alone, the way of life for other sovereign peoples. It can be resolved by United States dedication to the United Nations, as the sole hope of maintaining international peace by means of international law, all the energy and power and billions of dollars now being devoted to policies subversive of international authority. It can be resolved by the United States withdrawing its forces from Vietnam and pledging full respect and support for the international enforcement of terms of the Geneva Treaty of 1954, which guaranteed all Vietnam complete independence and freedom to determine its own future without the presence of any foreign troops, bases, or outside interference. That won't happen tomorrow.

Susan Sontag

A small nation of handsome people, ravished by twenty years of civil war, is being brutally and self-righteously slaughtered—in the name of freedom!—by the richest, most grotesquely overarmed, most powerful country in the world. America has become a criminal, sinister country—swollen with priggishness, numbed by affluence, bemused by the monstrous conceit that she has the mandate to dispose of the destiny of the world, *of life itself,* in terms of her own interests and jargon.

America's war on Vietnam makes me, for the first time in my life, ashamed of being an American. But that's unimportant.

I am in complete agreement with Bertrand Russell's statement that "Vietnam is an acid test for this generation of Western intellectuals."

Terry Southern

"Intervention" would seem to me rather weak semantics for the bombing of civilians . . . the use of napalm and herbicides . . . the destruction of villages, schools, hospitals, roads, bridges, crops . . . the massacre of women and children. I should have thought a somewhat stronger term—like "barbarism," "rape," or "pillage"—more correct.

Anyone who has had a casual or fleeting brush with mid-twentieth-century history, or even with the daily news of that period, knows that our "intervention," the so-called "American commitment in Vietnam," was more completely rigged than anything Al Capone ever dared to attempt. The most fitting analogy is the late great bout between Little Dave and Big Goliath— except that, in this one, the fix for Gol was supposed to be in. "Listen, kid . . ." says Davy's manager, "we decided to go for the price on Big Gol in the first." But Dave didn't buy it. "I can take him," says Dave— and if there is any justice (poetic) in the world, he'll do just that.

As for how to "resolve the conflict," there is only one conceivable way—and that is, with Johnson at the fore, quickly, silently, and with great stealth, to *slither* out, on our stomachs. Anything less would hardly be in character with our grotesquely reptilian behavior, and our very sick motives.

Stephen Spender

With feelings and instincts, I am opposed to the intervention of the United States in Vietnam. Most people I respect in America, especially the poets, are also opposed to it.

When one asks oneself how the intervention might end, one at once finds oneself an amateur and near ignoramus confronted by a whole variety of choices which range from saying that the Americans should withdraw immediately and unconditionally, to qualified approval or disapproval of what the Americans are at present doing. My own wish is that the Americans should stop the bombings, should—so far as this is possible—draw a line or establish an enclave which they declare it to be their intention to defend until they can reach agreement, preferably through the United Nations. In saying this, I think one has to admit that one does not know whether this "enclave policy" is militarily feasible. Some experts tell me it is. The Administration takes the view that they have considered such a policy and it is not feasible.

I had a private conversation with a Buddhist monk who has been received here [*] not only by the intellectuals but also by members of the Government, and who is greatly respected wherever he has been. I have not followed his public utterances but in private he has told me that he does not think the Americans should withdraw immediately. He thinks they should announce their intention to leave within a specific period and then negotiate. He added that he thinks the Vietcong would melt away if the Americans ceased to attack them, because what gives them unity is hatred of the "American occupiers." One would like to believe this, but how can one know?

Can one relate feelings and instincts to one's attempts to discover what is feasible and reasonable? I think one can at least say that there are positions which although they may seem justified by circumstances involve paying too heavy a price in blood and misery. The bombings certainly seem to me to be too heavy a price. I fear that a defeat would not just be an American humiliation. It would also be a great risk, and would lead almost certainly to massacres of those who have supported the Americans, and perhaps would lead also to other Vietnams in Asia. So it really seems a matter of weighing the dangers of defeat against the horrors already being perpetrated by the American attempts to win a victory. Somewhere between these lies the possibility of negotiation. I think that every effort should be made to negotiate; that the bombings do not create an atmosphere suitable for negotiation; and that if stopping the bombings makes some kind of defeat possible, then the price of such a defeat would be less great than of a victory won by sending another few hundreds of thousands of Americans to Vietnam, and extending the bombings, "escalation."

Enid Starkie

I am not so clear about the Vietnam affair as I was about the Spanish war. I am anti-Communist and do not approve of their way of infiltrating everywhere and of fostering strife for their own ends. It did seem, at the beginning, as if the Vietcong were guilty of aggres-

[*] Washington, D.C.—Eds.

sion, but I know that the matter is not entirely clear. From my limited knowledge, I suggest that they should not, with justice, win the war.

However, I have been against the bombing; during the Second World War I was also against saturation bombing, from whichever side, and I thought the atomic bomb attacks on Japan the worst single crimes of the war. I am also against any country interfering in the internal business of another country, and I find it hard to justify the American involvement in the Vietnam war at all. But of course, they are not the only people interfering.

I hardly feel qualified to make any pronouncements on the subject—except, in the vaguest terms, that I am against the bombing. But, although one is against violence, one should not allow a completely free hand to the other side.

Christina Stead

I believe the problems of Vietnam should be solved by the Vietnamese alone. The only other nations that might have any say in the matter are the signatories to the Geneva Convention. The United States was not a signatory. The division of Vietnam was admittedly temporary, an expedient, to permit South Vietnam to decide freely, without foreign control, whether it wished to be united with North Vietnam. A peaceful solution was envisaged by all parties.

The correct solution, I think, is to have no foreign troops in Vietnam, no military aid, no foreign installations. The South Vietnamese should be allowed to act in accord with the Geneva Conventions. Their decisions should be arrived at after absolute free speech and discussion of their own problems by the Vietnamese alone. It seems to me that we ourselves would ask for this; and any freedom-loving nation.

George Steiner

The war in Vietnam is an abomination. It is bringing hideous suffering and humiliation to an ancient culture. It is crippling and destroying human beings, many of them wholly uninvolved, and laying waste to their land. It is distorting important elements in American society. That society, in many ways the most generous and pragmatic on earth, is developing reflexes of brutality and self-deception which will damage not only itself but the many other nations which depend for their very survival on the sanity of American policies.

The war in Vietnam is doing damage, perhaps irreparable, to the fragile beginnings of a rational collaboration between the United States and the Soviet Union. It is, very probably, helping to harry China into some of its obvious paranoia.

In short: the thing is hideous and the stain of it is spreading.

But the way you put the question is an oversimplification. The intervention is not that of the United States alone. The conflict involves a plurality of legacies and interests, declared or covert. They range from those of France, still seeking a presence in Southeast Asia, to those of Thailand, of the Soviet Union, of the Buddhist community in Vietnam, etc. What would the consequences of American withdrawal—and my every instinct cries out for that solution—be? Civil war, accompanied by the almost inevitable decimation of the two million Catholics, many of them refugees from the North? A breakup into various regional, religious, political or ethnic subdivisions? Accommodation at the local level leading gradually to a "national front" regime?

Various forms of collectivist, centrally controlled societies, animated by fierce nationalism, often with a racist edge, are developing throughout Asia and Africa. The efforts of the United States to halt or police these new forms of human self-definition, or to place them under economic tutelage in some new mode of "progressive colonialism," are folly. Pressed too far they may lead to the final catastrophe of racial war.

But what is to be done right *now*, in late September 1966? Three steps are urgent: (1) reduction of the enormous American military establishment in Vietnam, an establishment bringing with it an entire complex of economic, psychological and technological vested interests; (2) cessation of the bombing of the North, if for no other reason than the fact that it is increasing Hanoi's will to fight; (3) an unequivocal declaration by the United States that it will negotiate with representatives of the Vietcong, and that it recognizes that the National Liberation Front is a crucial party to any settlement.

Where I differ from many of my radical colleagues, it is in this: I simply do not know whether these steps would, in fact, end the fighting. I cannot rule out entirely the possibility that Hanoi has only tenuous control over the Vietcong; or that America's immersion in this cruel morass, and the price America is now paying in terms of world opinion and support, are not distinctly to Peking's and Hanoi's strategic advantage. Do they want to stop the war, can they? Politics is said to be the art of the possible; but more often it looks as if it was a technique for making the intolerable go on.

I. F. Stone

1. Against.
   2. Negotiate with the NLF.

William Styron

I have been and still am utterly opposed to the participation of the United States in the Vietnam war. However, after having signed countless petitions and participated in protests and "read-ins," I am beginning to feel that writers and intellectuals are totally impotent in the face of these events. With only so much energy to expend, I consequently wonder if Mr. Eliot wasn't right when, in regard to the Spanish war, he maintained that "at least a few men of letters should remain isolated," and presumably tend to their work and their art.

Harvey Swados

1. Inasmuch as I am not an isolationist, I do support the intervention of the United States in Vietnam—in matters having to do with medicine, science, technology, humanistic research, and culture. I feel that it is not only the moral but the very practical duty of this nation to share to the very uttermost limits the fruits of its advanced technology with every nation which expresses the desire for such aid.

I hasten to add that I do not support the *military* intervention of the United States in Vietnam—nor did I support it when it was initiated under the guise of "military advice" by the crackpot realists of the New Frontier. The wild escalation undertaken by President Johnson is simply the logical extension of an originally idiotic notion: that communism is a theological-military enemy which must be extirpated with fire and sword. The espousal of this notion by those responsible for the formulation and conduct of American foreign policy means quite simply that (1) the United States is *the* major threat to world peace, and (2) we shall continue to live under sentence of mass annihilation, until such time as the American people learn to reject the notion as well as its proponents.

2. In my opinion the conflict in Vietnam should be resolved with the formation of a provisional Government composed of elements of the National Liberation Front, Buddhists, Catholics, and nonmilitary elements of the Saigon regime—such a provisional Government to hold nationwide elections under UN auspices. I am

not a partisan of victory for the Vietcong or for North Vietnam, nor would I contemplate with equanimity the imposition of a new tyranny upon a long-suffering people. Nevertheless it seems to me a *sine qua non* at this point that the United States get out of Vietnam militarily: gracefully if possible, gracelessly if need be, in order for a truce to be arranged and for the world to stop holding its breath.

Philip Toynbee

My attitude to the war in Vietnam is close to one of neutrality in that I think both sides almost equally wicked. I am, of course, against the disgusting savagery of the Americans, who are prepared to destroy a country rather than let it go Communist. I am also against the disgusting savagery of North Vietnam and the Vietcong, who are prepared to destroy a country rather than let it remain non-Communist. The ideologists fight; ordinary people suffer.

The only solution is an internationally supervised plebiscite in South Vietnam to decide whether they want their country to be Communist, anti-Communist or neutral.

Barbara W. Tuchman

1. I am against further active military intervention in Vietnam because its professed object—resistance of "aggression" by North Vietnam—is spurious and in any case not a vital interest of the US to the extent of sacrifice of American lives; and because its real object—containment of Chinese Communist expansion—requires rethinking of foreign and military policy.

2. I believe the present conflict might be resolved by careful, tactful and sophisticated negotiation carried on without public knowledge and through a third party such as the UN—though I suspect that the present Administration is too deeply committed to be significantly flexible and a final settlement may not be possible without a change of Administration—or at least of the Chief Executive.

Kenneth Tynan

1. Wholly against. Let's remember that it was the US who first brought foreign troops into South Vietnam, long before any infiltration from the North had begun.

When Hitler and Mussolini intervened in Spain to support a military rebellion, liberal opinion was rightly outraged. Why should it be otherwise when the US intervenes to prop up another military junta that has no more right to govern than Franco had?

2. At the moment (i.e., the summer of 1966), I suspect that the measures needed to end the war are the ones least likely to be taken, because they would involve President Johnson in the unpalatable necessity of losing face, not to mention votes. From Washington's point of view, to be Pacific-minded is apparently incompatible with being pacific-minded.

What probably *will* happen is a military victory for the US, at the Pyrrhic price of a devastated Vietnam and a permanent underground war in the South, which in turn would entail a permanent American military commitment. Of course, if Marshal Ky and the more predatory hawks have their way, the bombing of China cannot be ruled out. This would be a barbarous irrelevance: To borrow an analogy from I. F. Stone, the doyen of radical sanity in American journalism, it would be as if George III had invaded France in order to suppress the American War of Independence.

What *ought* to happen has been repeatedly spelled out by a band of devoted but increasingly despondent liberal observers. First, an immediate halt to the American bombing of North Vietnam and the American military build-up in the South. Second, a cease-fire negotiated with the NLF—not with Hanoi or Peking, because this is and always has been a war of national liberation, conducted first against the Japanese, then against the French and now against the Americans. Third, free elections in which all political groups take part, under the supervision of the International Control Commission or a similar body of demonstrable impartiality. Fourth, withdrawal of all American armed forces. But these proposals are too sensible to be probable.

It would help if Britain were to press for an instrumentation of the Geneva Agreements (which promised free elections); or, failing that, to lead a neutral bloc in dissociating itself from American entanglement in Vietnam. Even so, the key would still lie with American public opinion. The US does not have a history of losing wars. How can we convince them that in Vietnam an honorable withdrawal would be a resounding victory for global peace?

John Updike

Like most Americans I am uncomfortable about our military adventure in South Vietnam; but in honesty I wonder how much of the discomfort has to do with its high cost, in lives and money, and how much with its moral legitimacy. I do not believe that the Vietcong and Ho Chi Minh have a moral edge over us, nor do I believe that great powers can always avoid using their power. I am for our intervention if it does some good. Specifically, if it enables the people of South Vietnam to seek their own political future. It is absurd to suggest that a village in the grip of guerrillas has freely chosen, or that we owe it to history to bow before a wave of the future engineered by terrorists. The crying need is for genuine elections whereby the South Vietnamese can express their will. If their will is for communism, we should pick up our chips and leave. Until such a will is expressed, and as long as no willingness to negotiate is shown by the other side, I do not see that we can abdicate our burdensome position in South Vietnam.

Gore Vidal

1. I am opposed to American intervention in the Vietnamese civil war. We have neither the means nor the intelligence to maintain a world empire; unfortunately we do have the will, which means that we shall doubtless persist in such adventures and so be destroyed, along with a large portion of the human race. Biologically this may be a good thing, even inevitable; but one does not welcome the fiery end of even this poor civilization.

2. There is no resolution to the war as long as the American people are convinced that (1) the United States has never lost a war (despite the disaster of 1812, the draw in Korea), and (2) that once a thing is started it must be seen through to its logical end. In this case, the obliteration of Hanoi and a major war with China which we are bound to win since the United States has never lost a war, etc. To change the thinking or non-thinking of the majority is a task not about to be taken on by any politician who wants to be elected President. The best one can hope for is a fading away of the war as new crises distract us (there is, after all, Latin America to be saved from the menace of world communism). For myself, should the war in Vietnam continue after the 1968 election, a change in nationality will be the only moral response.

Rex Warner

1. I am, like most of my American friends, opposed to the intervention of the US in Vietnam.

2. I lack sufficient knowledge to attempt to say how

precisely the conflict should be resolved. Among those who seem to me to be thinking intelligently on the subject are Senator Fulbright, Walter Lippmann and General de Gaulle.

Sylvia Townsend Warner

I am against it. But if I were an out-and-out Communist I would, remembering the bracing effect of the wars of intervention against the USSR, be all for it.

By unregimented consultation between the North and South Vietnamese: no elections—they would be rigged—no outside pressure to speed up, and, ideally, all politicians, generals and religious leaders reduced to human size by having to earn their own livings.

The wounds of war heal by granulation: by mending roads and bridges, increasing livestock, growing more foodstuffs. Smuggling helps granulation (cf. Eire and Northern Ireland) so there may be something to be said for keeping a frontier.

Vernon Watkins

I write as one totally unskilled in politics, yet deeply concerned with human behavior. A country cannot be known until one enters it; and even then, under the camouflage of war, it is unrecognizable. One cannot understand war without either participating in it or experiencing its effects, and the participants themselves are driven to act blindly. War is a deforming agent, releasing vindictive forces and with them every kind of cruelty. I cannot therefore accept as good a policy which directs war and employs these forces.

If American aggression in Vietnam is not good, is it justified by expediency? Is one form of evil necessary to combat and subdue another? Aggression always springs from fear, and in war it is accompanied by the nobler instinct to protect one's own kind, to resist any tyranny which threatens them. Even this nobler instinct, which nearly always brings with it incalculable heroism, cannot excuse war.

I am asked what I advocate as a solution. The first necessity is to end the fighting, the second to arrive at a just peace. The withdrawal of American troops, far from humiliating their country, would be an act of international heroism. There is no justification for war today, or at any time in the future. Where evil exists it must be treated by peaceful means, and unjust imprisonment or persecution should be subject to international supervision. The wounds of violence cannot be healed by violence. An enlightened nation is one that hates war.

Alec Waugh

I do not think that you are justified in suggesting, as your question does, that the fighting in Vietnam is the result of the intervention of the USA.

In my opinion, American forces entered the conflict at the request of the South Vietnamese Government to protect South Vietnam from the intervention of North Vietnam in their affairs.

Auberon Waugh

From the shelter of our position as an opinionated, third-class power which is making no contribution to the war effort we may allow ourselves the luxury of criticizing the Americans' conduct of the war. To resent their presence in Vietnam seems to me suicidal. In any case, they have my unqualified admiration and gratitude for being there. Western intellectuals have their own predilections. The tragedy of Vietnam is that it should have misled so many warmhearted people of few intellectual pretensions—or left-wing sympathies—into support for a system which is unjust, incompetent and cruel.

The view that the NLF is an entirely indigenous growth seems to me as naïve as the opposite view, that it constitutes an invasion from the North. In neither case does it represent the aspirations of the South Vietnamese majority. No doubt many South Vietnamese would settle for a Communist tyranny rather than continue the war. They would probably settle for a return to French colonial rule, too. Few people are very brave when confronted by terrorism. Attempts to resist it often cause more havoc than the terrorists themselves. But that is no reason why terrorism should be allowed its way. Would anyone like to see the civil-rights issue settled by the same means? I do not see how the intentional killing of civilians can ever be justified, even as deterrent retaliation. If American bomber pilots are guilty of this, they are culpable, but it does not alter by one jot the justice of the war America is fighting. Chinese communism, through the Vietcong, is fighting a war of aggression. America is fighting a war of containment. Vietnam is the present point of contact between an almost immovable body and an almost irresistible force. It is a safety valve that may blow its top, but a safety valve nevertheless. For my own part, I am on the side of the immovable body.

There can never be a satisfactory conclusion so long as the aggressive dynamic exists. If America finally convinces North Vietnam that the game is not worth the candle, an identical war will break out somewhere along the Chinese border. Our only hope—and it is a selfish one—is that the next war will be to the north.

James Wellard

I am opposed to American intervention ("interference," of course, is the correct word) for political and social reasons. Though I am not a Communist (it is demeaning to have to say these things, but it has relevance to my argument), I believe some form of communism is both necessary and inevitable in ill-run countries in Asia, Africa, and probably South America. I have come to this conclusion from my travels and residence in such countries. Thus, we in the West, and notably the Americans, are trying to graft our advanced system of capitalism on tribal or feudal economies, with chaotic results. Everybody who has seen these "aid" programs in action knows that what happens is the rich get richer, the poor poorer, while corruption and tyranny reign supreme. Moreover, instead of anything changing for the better, everything old and bad and inefficient becomes more deeply entrenched. New ideas are scotched; young men who have broken with the feudal past are pushed aside. I found in Persia, for instance, that students who had acquired degrees and skills in the US universities were regarded with deep distrust and were given no opportunity to make a career for themselves. In brief, what we call democracy results in a hardening of the old outworn systems, well bolstered up with American money and arms. But underneath the surface, the young people—in particular, the intellectuals—and even the oppressed are waiting to blow the lid off, and until and unless we recognize this, we shall always have civil and international wars. If, on the other hand, we allowed backward peoples to change in their own way and at their own rate, they might in some cases opt for some sort of democratic regime (Tunisia is an example), or they might become quasi-Communist (Yugoslavia?). If I were a Moroccan worker or intellectual, I would consider communism the only solution, as the Americans in their day considered independence the only solution. So looking at these things historically, we see that it is impossible to stem the tide of change outside of total war, and annihilation of people does not prove anything except man's brutality and stupidity. Therefore, we should let Vietnam go Communist, as that would obviously be a better system than the old feudalism or the new military dictatorship. Such a solution would be no threat whatsoever to the West. The opposite view is based on hysteria.

Regarding the social implications—even more important than the political implications—the American war is destroying traditional morality and resulting in a new generation of thieves and thugs. Children's minds are being poisoned even more than their bodies maimed. Their inheritance after this is all over will be Western despair and cynicism, without any belief in religion, law, or morality. An old civilization will have been destroyed, and there will be nothing to replace it. Southeast Asia will be a more unsettled and more dangerous area of the world than before.

Insofar as the termination of the Vietnam war is concerned, I prefer to be as realistic as I tried to be concerning the facts of American intervention. Thus, the US cannot now withdraw unconditionally. She is entitled to lay down conditions and, I would say, has done so in a reasonable manner. In short, both sides have to withdraw, as in any fight. If, then, the US is honest and serious about withdrawal, and the North Vietnamese refuse to do so, the only solution is for the United Nations to send in a peace-keeping force (as in Korea) to force the North Vietnamese out. The territory should then be occupied by the UN in the manner of Libya after the war, or of the Israeli-Arab corridor at the present. To talk of free elections within the next two years is nonsense. The Vietnamese haven't the slightest idea what they will be voting for. The whole territory must therefore be kept "on ice" until the hatreds and destruction of the current war are ameliorated. There could be elections in, say, 1970— they would probably be farcical—and the West would have to accept the results. South Vietnam would no doubt become a socialist state. The point is this need be no threat to the West—at least, not in our lifetime—whereas the present condition can only lead to world war. I firmly believe "better red than dead" is a sound political and human maxim, though, as a writer, I would probably be more miserable under a Communist regime than I am now!

Arnold Wesker

Really what can one say? America's presence in Vietnam is wrong because it is unhelpful and it is suspect because she has managed to support a series of Governments she subsequently discovers to be corrupt.

No one but those familiar with all the details can answer how the conflict should be resolved. What can writers who have never been there know of the problems? They can only be depressed with the news of so much suffering, and angered by US tactics that appear to be crude and aggressive.

Are simple answers any solution? I would insist on American withdrawal of troops completely and hand the whole problem over to the United Nations. Then, after sufficient time had been allowed for both sides to settle into a semblance of routine and calm, nation-wide elections should be held. But who can know how possible this simple approach is? There must be all sorts of reasons why it can't happen in this way. And isn't it about time to ask how much of a "threat" communism is these days? De Gaulle seems to have asked it successfully.

Richard Wilbur

The new weapons have insured that the final stage of any big war must now be indiscriminate and suicidal. It is therefore time to consider abolishing the old Augustinian distinction between just and unjust warfare. But even if we reprieve that idea of the "just war" —the war for a good cause, in which likely gain outweighs likely loss, and the methods are relatively humane—it will not excuse our behavior in Vietnam. What we are doing is unjust on all counts, and Cardinal Spellman's endorsement is lamentable.

As I understand it, we have supported dictators of the landlord class against a legitimate popular reform movement, branding the latter "Communist" when we knew it was not, and forcing it at last to become so. We have claimed to believe, in the face of much contrary evidence, that "world communism" is unitary, and that it is our mission to suppress popular uprisings everywhere lest they go Communist. If we believe that, I fear that we are arrogant and wrong; if we do not believe that, then we are dishonest, and are guilty of recklessly advancing our line of national defense to the Chinese border. As for gain and loss, it is impossible to imagine what "victory" might be; but among the likely losses are the Vietnamese nation and the American sense of shame. Of the methods employed by the "allies" in this war—the crimes which we have committed or allowed—nothing need be said except that they alone would convict our enterprise of injustice.

The obstacle to our simply "getting out of Vietnam" is that we must protect from reprisals those with whom we have sided there. Consequently I think that we must stop bombing the North, reduce and concert our forces in holding positions, and ask the whole world's aid in securing direct negotiations with all concerned. It should be the least of our worries that some will take such action for weakness.

Angus Wilson

I have always been suspicious of For and Against questions. The Vietnam situation is bedeviled by them. All the protests I have been asked to support have been couched in terms which laid the blame completely upon the Americans, leaving no room for argument. I am myself convinced that the present refusal to negotiate must be blamed on Hanoi and her supporters, but I support what the Secretary General of the United Nations has said: namely, that peace can be restored only by a return to the Geneva Agreements and that, as a preparatory measure, it is necessary to start scaling down military operations, and to agree to discussions which include all the actual combatants. To assist toward this solution I have now come to think it vital that Britain should dissociate herself from United States policy—*not* in order thereby to make any judgment of the contestants, but to give us that vital degree of impartiality which alone can fit us for our role as co-chairman of the Geneva Conference.

If we could speak from such a position, we should have gone a long way toward bringing into the open any prevarication or hypocrisy in attitudes toward negotiations.

Colin Wilson

My attitude to Vietnam is ambiguous. *Given* the American premise that communism is a kind of cancer that must be fought at all costs, one can see that Johnson's attitude is only reasonable, and that it would involve serious loss of face for America to withdraw now. But I personally belong to those who, while not Communist, and opposed to all forms of totalitarianism, feel that the harsher and more repressive forms of communism were largely a result of the struggle it cost to establish them in Russia, China, Central Europe, etc. I believe, like Romain Gary, that America will now move steadily to the left, and the Communists to the right, and the present mutual mistrust will become a thing of the past. I have been in America and Russia, and have seen that each country has a totally false idea of the other, as a ruthless monster repressing its own people. The "ideological differences" between the East and West are not half so important as this total misunderstanding, which could be banished by honesty and good will. Given this premise, I can only feel that the war in Vietnam is an absurd business, another proof of Shaw's assertion that human beings take too long to grow up.

What can be done about it at this stage is another matter. One thing is absolutely certain: escalation is not merely wrong; it is futile, a waste of time. As my friend Robert Ardrey has pointed out in his studies of animal "territoriality," the defenders are always in the strongest position, psychologically speaking. And slow escalation is therefore pointless because every increase in American strength will result in an increase of the resistance of the Vietcong, who regard themselves as the defenders. If America had really wanted to settle the Vietnam situation successfully, then she should have thrown in all her present forces at the very beginning, and smashed the resistance, as Russia did with the Hungarian revolution. (I am not approving such a course, but speaking purely as an observer of animal behavior.) The slow escalation policy could prolong the war for another fifty years, in theory. So, in this matter, I am in agreement with the American moderates in believing that it is time to ease off, and start looking for settlements. There is *no* way to win, at this stage. And both sides are war-weary. This could be the moment to drop the fist-shaking, and take the first real step toward a truce with communism—by drawing China into the United Nations, for example.

Tom Wolfe

I predict your book will be marvelous stuff. Moralism is a foxhole for incompetents. I think everybody will be delighted to see all the writers screaming Yes! or No! or Arrrgggggh! and jumping in there. Best wishes.

Leonard Woolf

I am against the intervention of the US in Vietnam, but, in saying that, I wish to dissociate myself from the many people who use the Vietnam situation as an instrument of their anti-Americanism and/or Communist propaganda. I think the Americans should withdraw from Vietnam because their continued intervention is causing great loss and misery both to the Vietnamese and to themselves and is at the same time not achieving the object for which they intervened.

How the conflict should be resolved is a much more difficult question to answer. The first thing to do should be an attempt to get an agreement between the two sides—the Vietcong and the US—to cease hostilities and withdraw forces, leaving the Vietnamese to settle their own affairs, possibly with United Nations observers in the territory. I doubt whether agreement to this could be obtained or that the Communist forces could be trusted to carry it out. In the last resort I think the Americans should withdraw unilaterally and cut their losses.

The Contributors

Biographical entries contain the following information, wherever available: the author's name, date of birth, nationality, category of literature, list of works with dates of publication, and any other relevant particulars. The lists are not necessarily of the "most important" or latest books published by the author, but are intended to contain a selection of the works by which the contributor is most widely known.

The majority of these brief biographies were submitted to the authors for correction, although, for reasons of space and consistency, it did not always prove possible to adopt all their suggestions.

Nelson Algren (b. 1909): American novelist and short story writer. *Never Come Morning* (1942); *The Neon Wilderness* (1947); *The Man With the Golden Arm* (1949); *A Walk on the Wild Side* (1957); *Notes From a Sea Diary: Hemingway All the Way* (1965).

A. Alvarez (b. 1929): English poet and critic. *Stewards of Excellence* (1958); *The School of Donne* (1961); *The New Poetry* (1962); *Under Pressure: The Writer in Society: Eastern Europe and the USA* (1965).

Kingsley Amis (b. 1922): English novelist, poet, and critic. *Lucky Jim* (1954); *That Uncertain Feeling* (1955); *Take a Girl Like You* (1960); *New Maps of Hell* (1960); *One Fat Englishman* (1963); *The Anti-Death League* (1966).

Hannah Arendt (b. 1906): German-born historian and political scientist. *The Origins of Totalitarianism* (1951); *The Human Condition* (1958); *Between Past and Future* (1961); *On Revolution* (1963); *Eichmann in Jerusalem* (1963). Has lived in the US since 1941; naturalized 1950.

Giovanni Arpino (b. 1927): Italian novelist and children's writer. *A Crime of Honor* (1962); *The Novice* (1962).

W. H. Auden (b. 1907): English-born poet, essayist, and editor. *Poems* (1930); *The Orators* (1932); with Christopher Isherwood, *The Dog Beneath the Skin* (1935) and *The Ascent of F. 6* (1936); *Spain* (1937); *Collected Poetry* (1945); *The Age of Anxiety* (1947); *Collected Shorter Poems 1930–44* (1950); *Nones* (1951); *The Shield of Achilles* (1955); *Homage to Clio* (1960); *The Dyer's Hand* (1962); *About the House* (1965). Emigrated to the US in 1939; became an American citizen in 1946.

A. J. Ayer (b. 1910): English philosopher. *Language, Truth and Logic* (1936); *The Foundations of Empirical Knowledge* (1940); *Philosophical Essays* (1954); *The Problem of Knowledge* (1956); *The Concept of a Person and Other Essays* (1963). Wykeham Professor of Logic at Oxford.

James Baldwin (b. 1924): American novelist, essayist, and playwright. *Go Tell It on the Mountain* (1953); *Giovanni's Room* (1956); *Notes of a Native Son* (1955); *Nobody Knows My Name* (1961); *Another Country* (1962); *The Fire Next Time* (1963); *Blues for Mr. Charlie* (1964); *Going to Meet the Man* (1965).

George Barker (b. 1913): English poet and novelist. *The Dead Seagull* (1950); *Collected Poems 1930–65* (1965). Professor of English Literature at Imperial Tohoku University, Japan, 1939.

Vernon Bartlett (b. 1894): English publicist, journalist, and broadcaster. With R. C. Sherriff, *Journey's End* (1930); *Struggle for Africa* (1953); *Report From Malaya* (1954); *And Now, Tomorrow* (1960). Independent Progressive Member of Parliament, 1938–50. Lives in Italy.

Simone de Beauvoir (b. 1908): French novelist, essayist, philosopher, and playwright. *The Second Sex* (1953); *She Came to Stay* (1954); *All Men Are Mortal* (1955); *The Mandarins* (1956); *The Long March* (1958); *Memoirs of a Dutiful Daughter* (1959); *The Prime of Life* (1962); *The Force of Circumstance* (1965); *A Very Easy Death* (1966).

S. N. Behrman (b. 1893): American playwright, scriptwriter, and biographer. *Serena Blandish* (1928); *Biography* (1933); *Rain From Heaven* (1935); *Amphitryon 38* (1938); *No Time for Comedy* (1939); *The Pirate* (1942); *Duveen* (1952); with Joshua Logan, *Fanny* (1954); *Portrait of Max* (1960); *Suspended Drawing Room* (1965). Films: *Queen Christina, A Tale of Two Cities, Me and the Colonel.*

Nathaniel Benchley (b. 1915): American novelist, short story writer, and journalist. *Side Street* (1950); *Robert Benchley* (1955); *The Off Islanders* (1961); *A Winter's Tale* (1964); *A Firm Word or Two* (1965); *The Monument* (1966).

Isaiah Berlin (b. 1909): English philosopher, historian, and critic. *Karl Marx* (1939); *The Hedgehog and the Fox* (1953); *Historical Inevitability* (1954); *The Age of Enlightenment* (1956); *Two Concepts of Liberty* (1958); *The Life and Opinions of Moses Hess* (1959); *Mr. Churchill in 1940* (1964). Served at British Embassies, Washington and Moscow, 1942–46; philosophy tutor at Oxford University, 1932–40 and 1950–57; formerly Fellow of All Souls College and New College, Oxford. Chichele Professor of Social and Political Theory at Oxford, 1957–67; President of Wolfson College, Oxford.

Giuseppe Berto (b. 1914): Italian novelist, short story writer, and scriptwriter. *The Sky Is Red* (1948); *Works of God* (1950); *The Brigand* (1951); *The Incubus* (1966).

Mongo Beti (b. 1932): Cameroonian novelist. *Le Pauvre Christ de Bomba* (1956); *Mission Terminée* (1957); *Le Roi Miraculé* (1958).

Edmund Blunden (b. 1896): English poet, essayist, critic, and editor. *Undertones of War* (1930); *Poems 1930–40* (1940); *Poems of Many Years* (1957). Professor of English Literature, Tokyo University, 1924–27; with UK Liaison Commission, Tokyo, 1948–50; Honorary Member of the Japan Academy.

Hector Bolitho (b. 1897): New Zealand-born historian, biographer, and novelist. *Twelve Against the Gods* (1929); *A Biographer's Notebook* (1950); *Jinnah, Creator of Pakistan* (1954); *Albert, Prince Consort* (1964). Lives in Britain.

Heinrich Böll (b. 1917): West German novelist, essayist, and short story writer. *Adam, Where Art Thou?* (1955); *Billiards at Half-past Nine* (1962); *Absent Without Leave* (1965); *18 Stories* (1966).

Robert Bolt (b. 1924): English playwright. *Flowering Cherry* (1958); *A Man for All Seasons* (1960); wrote screen play for *Lawrence of Arabia* (1962), *Dr. Zhivago* (1965), and *A Man for All Seasons* (1966). He played a leading role in demonstrations against the use of nuclear weapons and, together with Bertrand Russell and other notable Englishmen, was sentenced in 1961 to one month's imprisonment.

Kay Boyle (b. 1903): American poet, novelist, and short story writer. *Avalanche* (1944); *Thirty Stories* (1946); *1939* (1948); *Three Short Novels* (1958); *Generation Without Farewell* (1959); *Collected Poems* (1962). Visited Cambodia in August 1966 on a fact-finding mission.

John Braine (b. 1922): English novelist. *Room at the Top* (1957); *From the Hand of the Hunter* (1959); *Life at the Top* (1962); *The Jealous God* (1964).

John Malcolm Brinnin (b. 1916): American poet, literary critic, and editor. *Dylan Thomas in America* (1955); *The Third Rose: Gertrude Stein and Her World* (1959); *Selected Poems* (1963). Professor of English, Boston University.

Vera Brittain (b. 1896): English novelist and essayist. *Testament of Youth* (1933); *Testament of Friendship: The Story of Winifred Holtby* (1933); *Humiliation With Honour* [on pacifism] (1942).

Brigid Brophy (b. 1929): English novelist and essayist. *Hackenfeller's Ape* (1953); *Black Ship to Hell* (1962); *Flesh* (1962); *Mozart the Dramatist* (1964); *The Snow Ball* (1964); *Don't Never Forget* (1967).

Robert Brustein (b. 1927): American critic and educator. *The Theatre of Revolt* (1964); ed., *The Plays and Prose of Strindberg* (1964); *Seasons of Discontent* (1965). Dean of Yale University School of Drama and Professor of English since July 1966.

William F. Buckley, Jr. (b. 1925): American journalist and author. *God and Man at Yale* (1951); *Up From Liberalism* (1959); *The Unmaking of a Mayor* (1966). Editor of *The National Review*. Candidate for Mayor of New York City, 1966.

James Burnham (b. 1905): American philosopher and political scientist. *The Managerial Revolution* (1941); *The Struggle for the World* (1947); *Suicide of the West* (1964).

William S. Burroughs (b. 1914): American novelist. *Junkie* (1953), *Naked Lunch* (1959); *The Soft Machine* (1961); *The Ticket That Exploded* (1962); *Dead Fingers Talk* (1963); *Nova Express* (1964). Lives in England and France.

Italo Calvino (b. 1923): Italian novelist and short story writer. *The Path to the Nest of Spiders* (1957); *The Baron in the Trees* (1959); *Italian Fables* (1959); *The Nonexistent Knight, and the Cloven Viscount* (1962).

James Cameron (b. 1911): Scottish author, journalist, and foreign correspondent. *Touch of the Sun* (1950); *Man-*

darin Red: A Journey Behind the Bamboo Curtain (1955); *The African Revolution* (1961); *Here Is Your Enemy* [an account of a journey to North Vietnam] (1966). He has worked extensively in Asia, and in the early part of 1966 was the first British journalist in North Vietnam for many years.

Camilo José Cela (b. 1916): Spanish novelist, essayist, and short story and travel writer. *Hive* (1953); *Ávila* (1964); *The Family of Pascual Duarte* (1964); *Journey to the Alcarria* (1964).

Paddy Chayefsky (b. 1923): American playwright and scriptwriter. *Television Plays* (1956); *The Middle of the Night* (1957); *The Goddess* (1958); *The Tenth Man* (1960); *Gideon* (1961); *The Passion of Josef D.* (1964); writer and associate producer of films: *Marty* (1955); *The Bachelor Party* (1957); *The Middle of the Night* (1959); *The Americanization of Emily* (1964).

John Cheever (b. 1912): American novelist and short story writer. *The Way Some People Live* (1942); *The Enormous Radio and Other Stories* (1953); *The Wapshot Chronicle* (1957); *The Housebreaker of Shady Hill* (1959); *Some People, Places and Things That Will Not Appear in My Next Novel* (1961); *The Wapshot Scandal* (1964); *The Brigadier and the Golf Widow* (1964).

Haakon Chevalier (b. 1902): American novelist, translator, and critic. *The Ironic Temper: Anatole France and His Time* (1932); *The Man Who Would Be God* (1959); *Oppenheimer: The Story of a Friendship* (1966). French interpreter at the Allied trials of German war criminals, Nuremberg, 1945–6. Has lived in France since 1950.

Robert Conquest (b. 1917): English poet, critic, and writer on Soviet affairs. *Poems* (1955); *The Soviet Deportation of Nationalities* (1960); *Common Sense About Russia* (1960); *Courage of Genius: The Pasternak Affair* (1961); *Power and Policy in the USSR* (1961); *Between Mars and Venus* (1962); *Russia After Khrushchev* (1965).

Robert Creeley (b. 1926): American poet and novelist. *For Love: Poems, 1950–60* (1962); *The Island* (1963); *The Gold Diggers* (1965); *Words* (1967).

Robert Crichton (b. 1925): American author. *The Great Impostor* (1959); *The Rascal and the Road* (1961); *The Secret of Santa Vittoria* (1966).

Rupert Croft-Cooke (b. 1903): English novelist, playwright, biographer, and writer of books on travel, food, wine, the circus, and Gypsies. *The Man in Europe Street* (1938); *Willkie* (1948); *The Verdict of You All* (1955); *Seven Thunders* (1956). Lives in Tangier.

David Daiches (b. 1912): British critic. *The Novel and the Modern World* (1939); *Robert Burns* (1951); *Milton* (1955); *A Critical History of English Literature* (1960). Professor of English and Dean of the School of English and American Studies at the University of Sussex.

Len Deighton (b. 1929): English novelist. *The Ipcress File* (1963); *Funeral in Berlin* (1964); *The Billion Dollar Brain* (1966); *An Expensive Place To Die* (1967).

Babette Deutsch (b. 1895): American poet, critic, novelist, children's writer, and translator. *The Reader's Shakespeare* (1946); *Poetry in Our Time* (1952); *Poetry Handbook* (1957); *Coming of Age* (1959); *Collected Poems, 1919–62* (1963).

Isaac Deutscher (1907–67): Polish-born historian and journalist. *Stalin: A Political Biography* (1949); a 3-volume biography of Trotsky (1954–63); *Ironies of History* (1966). Expelled from the Polish Communist Party in 1932 for anti-Stalinist activities and emigrated to England. G. M. Trevelyan Lecturer, Cambridge University, 1966–67. Isaac Deutscher died August 19th, 1967.

Peter De Vries (b. 1910): American novelist. *No, But I Saw the Movie* (1952); *The Tunnel of Love* (1954); *Comfort Me With Apples* (1956); *Tents of Wickedness* (1959); *Through Fields of Clover* (1961); *Reuben, Reuben* (1964); *Let Me Count the Ways* (1965).

Daphne du Maurier (b. 1907): English novelist and playwright. *Jamaica Inn* (1936); *The du Mauriers* (1937); *Rebecca* (1938); *Frenchman's Creek* (1941); *The King's General* (1945); *My Cousin Rachel* (1951); *Mary Anne* (1954); *The Scapegoat* (1957); *The Flight of the Falcon* (1965).

Nell Dunn (b. 1936): English author. *Up the Junction* (1963); *Talking to Women* (1965); *Poor Cow* (1967).

Richard Eberhart (b. 1904): American poet, playwright, and literary critic. Ed., with S. Rodman, *War and the Poet* (1945); *Collected Poems, 1930–60* (1960); *Collected Verse Plays* (1962); *Selected Poems, 1930–65* (1965). Professor of English and Poet-in-Residence, Dartmouth College.

Richard Ellmann (b. 1918): American literary critic and biographer. *Yeats: The Man and the Masks* (1948); *The Identity of Yeats* (1954); *James Joyce* (1959). Professor of English, Northwestern University.

William Empson (b. 1906): English critic and poet. *Seven Types of Ambiguity* (1930); *Collected Poems* (1949); *Some Versions of Pastoral* (1950); *The Structure of Complex Words* (1951); *Milton's God* (1962). Professor of English Literature at Tokyo, 1931–34; BBC Chinese editor, 1941–46; Professor in Western Language Department, Peking National University, 1937–39, 1947–52; now Professor of English Literature, Sheffield University.

Jules Feiffer (b. 1929): American cartoonist, novelist, and playwright. *Sick, Sick, Sick* (1958); *Passionella, and Other Stories* (1959); *Harry, the Rat with Women* (1963); *The Great Comic Book Heroes* (1965); *Little Murders* (1967).

Lawrence Ferlinghetti (b. 1920): American poet, novelist, and editor. *Picture of the Gone World* (1955); *A Coney Island of the Mind* (1958); *Her* (1960); *Starting From San Francisco* (1961); *Unfair Arguments With Existence* (1963); *Routines* (1964).

Leslie A. Fiedler (b. 1917): American novelist, poet, literary critic, essayist, and short story writer. *An End to Innocence* (1955); *Love and Death in the American Novel* (1960); *No! in Thunder* (1960); *Pull Down Vanity* (1962); *The Second Stone* (1963); *Waiting for the End* (1964); *Back to China* (1965); *The Last Jew in America* (1966). Professor of English, State University of New York at Buffalo.

Gabriel Fielding (b. 1916): English novelist. *In the Time of Greenbloom* (1957); *Eight Days* (1959); *Through Streets Broad and Narrow* (1960); *The Birthday King* (1963); *Gentlemen in Their Season* (1966). Professor of English, Washington State University.

Constantine FitzGibbon (b. 1919): American citizen and English novelist and translator. *The Arabian Bird* (1949); *When the Kissing Had to Stop* (1960); *The Life of Dylan Thomas* (1965). Lives in England.

John Fowles (b. 1926): English novelist. *The Collector* (1963); *The Aristos: A Self-Portrait in Ideas* (1964); *The Magus* (1965).

Pamela Frankau (1908–67): English novelist. *A Wreath for the Enemy* (1954); *Sing for Your Supper* (1963); *Slaves of the Lamp* (1965); *Over the Mountains* (1967). Pamela Frankau died on June 8th, 1967.

Northrop Frye (b. 1912): Canadian critic, essayist, editor, and educator. *Fearful Symmetry: A Study of William Blake* (1947); *Sound and Poetry* (1956); *Anatomy of Criticism* (1957); *Fables of Identity* (1963); *Romanticism Reconsidered* (1963); *T. S. Eliot* (1963); *The Well-tempered Critic* (1963); *The Educated Imagination* (1964); *A Natural Perspective* (1965); *The Return of Eden* (1965). University Professor, U. of Toronto.

David Garnett (b. 1892): English novelist and critic. *Lady Into Fox* (1922); *A Man in the Zoo* (1924); *War in the Air* (1940); *The Golden Echo* (1953); *The Flowers of the Forest* (1955); *Aspects of Love* (1955); *A Shot in the Dark* (1958); *Familiar Faces* (1962); *Two by Two* (1963).

Allen Ginsberg (b. 1926): American poet. *Howl and Other Poems* (1956); *Empty Mirror* (1961); *Kaddish and Other Poems 1958–60* (1961); *Reality Sandwiches 1953–60* (1963).

Paul Goodman (b. 1911): American essayist, editor, educator, and novelist. *Kafka's Prayer* (1947); with Percival Goodman, *Communitas* (1947); with others, *Gestalt Therapy* (1951); *The Structure of Literature* (1954); *The Empire City* (1959); *Growing Up Absurd* (1960); *Utopian Essays and Practical Proposals* (1962); *Making Do* (1963); *Compulsory Mis-education* (1964); *People or Personnel* (1965).

Robert Graves (b. 1895): English poet, novelist, short story writer, translator, and historian. *Good-bye to All That* (1929); *I, Claudius* (1934); *Claudius, the God* (1934); *Count Belisarius* (1938); *Wife to Mr. Milton* (1942); *Hercules, My Shipmate* (1944); *The White Goddess* (1947); *The Golden Ass* (1951); with Joshua Podro, *The Nazarene Gospel Restored* (1953); *The Greek Myths* (1955); *Collected Short Stories* (1965); *Collected Poems* (1965). Professor of English, Royal Egyptian University, Cairo, 1926. Has lived in Majorca since 1929. Professor of Poetry at Oxford 1961–66.

Graham Greene (b. 1904): English novelist, short story writer, and playwright. *Brighton Rock* (1938); *The Power and the Glory* (1940); *The Heart of the Matter* (1948); *The Third Man* (1950); *The End of the Affair* (1951); *The Living Room* (1953); *The Potting Shed* (1957); *Our Man in Havana* (1958); *The Complaisant Lover* (1959); *A Burnt-out Case* (1961); *The Comedians* (1966); *May We Borrow Your Husband? and Other Comedies of the Sexual Life* (1967). Between 1952 and 1955, he went to Indochina three times as a correspondent for *The Sunday Times* and *Le Figaro*, and one result was his novel *The Quiet American* (1956). He lives in France.

Geoffrey Grigson (b. 1905): English poet, critic, editor, and broadcaster. *Collected Poems* (1963); *Poets in Their Pride* (1964). State Department touring guest, USA, 1951.

Stuart Hampshire (b. 1914): English philosopher and critic. *Spinoza* (1956); *Thought and Action* (1960); *Freedom of the Individual* (1965). Professor of Philosophy, Princeton University.

Roy Harrod (b. 1900): English economist and biographer. *International Economics* (1933); *Towards a Dynamic Economics* (1948); *The Life of J. M. Keynes* (1951); *Foundations of Inductive Logic* (1956); *Reforming the World's Money* (1965).

Joseph Heller (b. 1923): American novelist. *Catch-22* (1961).

Nat Hentoff (b. 1925): American journalist, novelist, and essayist. Ed., with N. Shapiro, *Hear Me Talkin' to Ya* (1955); ed., *The Jazz Makers* (1957); with Albert McCarthy, *Jazz*, (1959); *The Jazz Life* (1961); *The Peace Agitator* (1963); *The New Equality* (1965); *Jazz Country* (1965); *Call the Keeper* (1966); *Our Children Are Dying* (1966); ed., *Essays of A. J. Muste* (1967).

Thor Heyerdahl (b. 1914): Norwegian explorer and writer on anthropology. *Kon-Tiki* (1950); *American Indians in the Pacific* (1953); *Aku-Aku* (1957); *The Archaeology of Easter Island* (2 v., 1961–65); *Vanished Civilizations* (1963). Lives in Italy.

Christopher Hill (b. 1912): English historian. *The English Revolution, 1640* (1940); *Lenin and the Russian Revolution* (1947); *The Century of Revolution, 1603–1714* (1961); *Intellectual Origins of the English Revolution* (1965).

David Holbrook (b. 1923): English poet, novelist, critic, educational writer, and teacher. *English for Maturity* (1962); *Against the Cruel Frost* (1963); *The Secret Places* (1964); *English for the Rejected* (1964); *Flesh Wounds* (1966); *Object Relations* (1967).

Vyvyan Holland (b. 1886): English author and translator. *Son of Oscar Wilde* (1954); *Oscar Wilde: A Pictorial Biography* (1960); *Goya: A Pictorial Biography* (1961); *Time Remembered* (1966); and many translations into English from French, Spanish, Italian, and German.

Elspeth Huxley (b. 1907): English novelist and writer and broadcaster on African affairs. *White Man's Country* (1935); *Race and Politics in Kenya* (1944); *The Flame Trees of Thika: Memories of an African Childhood* (1959); *A New Earth* (1960); *On the Edge of the Rift* (1963); *With Forks and Hope* (1964); *Back Street New Worlds* (1965).

Hammond Innes (b. 1913): Scottish novelist and travel writer. *The Lonely Skier* (1947); *The White South* (1949); *Campbell's Kingdom* (1952); *The Wreck of the Mary Deare* (1956); *The Land God Gave to Cain* (1958); *Harvest of Journeys* (1960); *Atlantic Fury* (1962); *Strode Venturer* (1965).

Pamela Hansford Johnson (b. 1912): English novelist and critic. *This Bed Thy Center* (1935); *An Avenue of Stone* (1947); *The Sea and the Wedding* (1956); *The Unspeakable Skipton* (1959); *The Humbler Creation* (1960); *An Error of Judgement* (1962); *The Art of Thomas Wolfe* (1963); *Night and Silence* (1963); *Cork Street* (1965); *On Iniquity* (1967).

Uwe Johnson (b. 1934): West German novelist. *Speculations About Jakob* (1963); *Two Views* (1966); *The Third Book About Achim* (1967).

James Jones (b. 1921): American novelist and short story writer. *From Here to Eternity* (1951); *Some Came Running* (1958); *The Pistol* (1959); *The Thin Red Line* (1962); *Go to the Widow-Maker* (1967). Has lived in France since 1958.

Stanley Kauffmann (b. 1916): American novelist, playwright, and critic. *Tightrope* (1952); *A Change of Climate* (1954); *The Very Man* (1956); *A World on Film* (1966).

Walter Kaufmann (b. 1921): German-born philosopher, critic, poet, and translator. *Nietzsche* (1950); *Critique of Religion and Philosophy* (1958); *Existentialism from Dostoyevsky to Sartre* (1956); *From Shakespeare to Existentialism* (1959); *The Faith of a Heretic* (1961); *Religion from Tolstoy to Camus* (1961); *Cain, and Other Poems* (1962); *Hegel* (1965); ed. and translator of *Twenty German Poets* (1962). Came to US 1939, naturalized American 1944. Professor of Philosophy, Princeton University.

Yuri Kazakov (b. 1927): Russian short story writer. *The Blue and the Green* (1957); *At the Station* (1959); *On the Way* (1961); *Going to Town and Other Stories* (1964); *Selected Short Stories* (1964); *Two in December* (1966). Kazakov is described in *Who's Who in the USSR, 1965–66* as a "controversial writer whose works have frequently been criticized."

Frank Kermode (b. 1919): English literary critic and editor. *Romantic Image* (1957); *Puzzles and Epiphanies* (1962); *The Sense of an Ending* (1967). Following revelations, in May 1967, that *Encounter* had been financed by the Central Intelligence Agency, Kermode resigned from the co-editorship of the journal. Winterstoke Professor of English, University of Bristol.

Bernard Kops (b. 1926): English poet, novelist, and playwright. *The Hamlet of Stepney Green* (1958); *Poems and Songs* (1958); *The Dream of Peter Mann* (1960); *The World Is a Wedding* (1963); *Yes From No-Man's Land* (1965); *Enter Solly Gold* (1965); *The Dissent of Dominic Shapiro* (1967).

Jerzy Kosinski (b. 1933): Polish-born novelist. *The Painted Bird* (1965). Under pseud. Joseph Novak, *The Future is Ours, Comrade: Conversations With the Russians* (1960); *No Third Path: A Study of Collective Behavior* (1962). Has lived in the US since 1958; naturalized in 1965.

Mark Lane (b. 1927): American lawyer, author, and lecturer. *Rush to Judgment: A Critique of the Warren Commission's Inquiry Into the Murders of President J. F. Kennedy, J. D. Tippit and L. H. Oswald* (1966). Former member of the New York State Legislature.

Marghanita Laski (b. 1915): English novelist and critic. *Little Boy Lost* (1949); *The Victorian Chaise-Longue* (1954); *The Offshore Island* (1959); *Ecstasy* (1962).

Doris Lessing (b. Persia 1919): Rhodesian novelist, short story writer, and playwright. *The Grass Is Singing* (1950); *This Was the Old Chief's Country* (1952); *The Habit of Loving* (1958); *In Pursuit of the English* (1961); *The Golden Notebook* (1962); *A Man and Two Women* (1963); a novel sequence, *Children of Violence* (1964–); *African Stories* (1965). Has lived in England since 1949.

Denise Levertov (b. 1923): English-born poet, naturalized American. *The Double Image* (1946); *Here and Now* (1956); *Overland to the Islands* (1958); *With Eyes at the Back of Our Heads* (1960); *Jacob's Ladder* (1961); *O Taste and See* (1964); *The Sorrow Dance* (1967).

Jakov Lind (b. 1927): Austrian-born novelist and playwright. *Soul of Wood and Other Stories* (1964); *Landscape in Concrete* (1966). Lives in England.

Eric Linklater (b. 1889): Scottish novelist, biographer, and military historian. *Poet's Pub* (1930); *Juan in America* (1931); *Juan in China* (1937); *Private Angelo* (1946); *The Campaign in Italy* (1951); *Our Men in Korea*, an official account of the part played by the Commonwealth forces in the Korean war (1952); *The Conquest of England* (1966).

Richard Llewellyn (b. 1906): Welsh novelist, playwright, and short story writer. *How Green Was My Valley* (1939); *None but the Lonely Heart* (1943); *A Few Flowers for Shiner* (1950); *A Flame for Doubting Thomas* (1953); *Up, Into the Singing Mountain* (1963); *Down Where the Moon Is Small* (1966).

Colin MacInnes (b. 1914): English novelist. *June in Her Spring* (1952); *City of Spades* (1957); *Absolute Beginners* (1959); *Mr. Love and Justice* (1960).

Marshall McLuhan (b. 1911): Canadian author, critic, and editor. *The Mechanical Bride* (1951); *The Gutenberg Galaxy* (1962); *Understanding Media* (1964); with Q. Fiore, *The Medium Is the Massage* (1967). Professor of English at the University of Toronto and Director of the Center for Culture and Technology. Schweitzer Professor of Humanities at Fordham University, 1967–.

Salvador de Madariaga (b. 1886): Spanish man of letters. *Christopher Columbus* (1939); *Hernán Cortés* (1941); *Bolívar* (1952); *Portrait of Europe* (1952). In 1931 he was Spanish Ambassador to the US, and from 1932 to 1934 Spanish Ambassador to France. Lives in England.

Norman Mailer (b. 1923): American novelist, essayist, and playwright. *The Naked and the Dead* (1948); *Barbary Shore* (1951); *The Deer Park* (1955); *The White Negro* (1957); *Advertisements for Myself* (1959); *The Presidential Papers* (1963); *An American Dream* (1965); *Cannibals and Christians* (1966).

Olivia Manning: English novelist. *The Remarkable Expedition* (1947); *The Doves of Venus* (1955); *My Husband Cartwright* (1956); *Friends and Heroes* (1965).

Herbert Marcuse (b. 1898): German-born philosopher and political scientist. *Reason and Revolution* (1941); *Eros and Civilization: A Philosophical Inquiry into Freud* (1956); *Soviet Marxism: A Critical Analysis* (1958); *One Dimensional Man* (1964). He was naturalized and has lived in the US since 1934. Professor of Philosophy at the University of California, San Diego.

Kingsley Martin (b. 1897): English political journalist, historian, and editor. *The Triumph of Lord Palmerston* (1924); *French Liberal Thought in the 18th Century* (1929); *The Crown and the Establishment* (1962). Editor of *The New Statesman and Nation*, 1931–60.

Gavin Maxwell (b. 1914): Scottish writer on natural history and travel. *Harpoon at a Venture* (1952); *A Reed Shaken by the Wind* (1957); *Ring of Bright Water* (1961); *Rocks Remain* (1963); *The House of Elrig* (1965); *Lords of the Atlas* (1966).

Thomas Merton (b. 1915): American poet, philosopher, and religious writer. *Seven Storey Mountain* (1948); *Seeds of Contemplation* (1949); *The Sign of Jonas* (1953); *Bread in the Wilderness* (1953); *No Man Is an Island* (1955); *The Silent Life* (1957); *Selected Poems* (1959); *Seeds of Destruction* (1964); *Seasons of Celebration* (1965). Member of the Order of Cistercians of the Strict Observance.

James A. Michener (b. 1907): American novelist. *Tales of the South Pacific* (1947) [the 1949 musical *South Pacific* was based on this work]; *The Voice of Asia* (1951); *The Bridges at Toko-Ri* (1953); *Sayonara* (1954); *Bridge at Andan* (1957); *Hawaii* (1959); *Caravans* (1963); *The Source* (1965). Naval historian in the South Pacific, 1944–46.

Arthur Miller (b. 1915): American playwright, essayist, novelist, and short story writer. *Focus* (1945); *All My Sons* (1947); *Death of a Salesman* (1949); *The Crucible* (1953); *A View From the Bridge* (1955); *Collected Plays* (1958); *The Misfits* (1961); *After the Fall* (1963); *Incident at Vichy* (1964); *I Don't Need You Any More* (1967).

Naomi Mitchison (b. 1897): Scottish novelist and children's writer. *The Conquered* (1923); *The Corn King and the Spring Queen* (1931); *Memoirs of a Spacewoman* (1962); *When We Become Men* [on Bechuanaland] (1964).

Jessica Mitford (b. 1917): English-born author. *Lifeitselfmanship* (1956); *Daughters and Rebels* (1960); *The American Way of Death* (1963). Has lived in the US since 1939; naturalized in 1944.

Nancy Mitford (b. 1904): English novelist, biographer, and translator. *The Pursuit of Love* (1945); *Love in a Cold Climate* (1949); *The Blessing* (1951); *Madame de Pompadour* (1954); *Noblesse Oblige* (1957); *Voltaire in Love* (1958); *The Water Beetle* (1963); *The Sun King* (1966).

Nicholas Monsarrat (b. 1910): English novelist and short story writer. *The Cruel Sea* (1951); *The Tribe That Lost Its Head* (1956); *Life Is a Four-Letter Word* (1967).

Luís de Sttau Monteiro (b. 1926): Portuguese playwright, short story writer, and novelist. *Rules of the Game* (1961); *O Barão* (1964); *Peças em um Acto* (1966). His first play, *Felizmente Hà Luar* (1961), which won the Grand Prémio of the Portuguese Theater and has gone through five editions, is forbidden to be performed by the Government department of political censorship. Two subsequent plays were suppressed in 1963 and 1964. A few days after sending his statement on Vietnam for the present work, a volume appeared containing two one-act plays, the first of which is a bitter satire upon war and armies in general. Shortly after publication the book was seized by the political police, the publishers were closed down, and the author was arrested. Since November 24, 1966, de Sttau Monteiro has been held in the political prison of Caxias. This is the second time that he has been detained. He was held for nearly a month in 1962, after the attempt to storm the army barracks in the southern city of Beja had failed.

Marianne Moore (b. 1887): American poet. *Selected Poems* (1935); *Collected Poems* (1951); trans., *The Fables of La Fontaine* (1954); *Predilections* (1955); *Like a Bulwark* (1956); *O, To Be A Dragon* (1959); *A Marianne Moore Reader* (1961); *Tell Me, Tell Me* (1966).

Alan Moorehead (b. 1910): Australian travel writer, journalist, and military historian. *African Trilogy* (1944); *The Traitors* (1952); *Gallipoli* (1956); *The Russian Revolution* (1958); *No Room in the Ark* (1959); *The White Nile* (1961); *The Blue Nile* (1962); *The Fatal Impact* (1966). Lives in Europe.

Dom Moraes (b. 1938): Indian poet and journalist. *Green Is the Grass* (1951); *A Beginning* (1957); *Gone Away* (1960); *John Nobody* (1965); *Poems 1955–65* (1966). Has lived in England since 1956.

Raymond Mortimer (b. 1895): English literary critic and essayist. *Channel Packet* (1942).

Malcolm Muggeridge (b. 1903): English author, journalist, critic, and broadcaster. *Winter in Moscow* (1934); *The Earnest Atheist: Samuel Butler* (1936); *The Thirties in Great Britain* (1940); *An Affair of the Heart* (1961); *The Most of Malcolm Muggeridge* (1966).

Lewis Mumford (b. 1895): American author. *Herman Melville* (1929); *The Brown Decades* (1931); *Technics and Civilization* (1934); *The Culture of Cities* (1938); *Men Must Act* (1939); *Faith for Living* (1940); *The Conduct of Life* (1951); *Art and Technics* (1952); *In the Name of Sanity* (1954); *From the Ground Up* (1956); *The City in History* (1961); *The Highway and the City* (1963); *The Myth of The Machine* (1967).

Iris Murdoch (b. 1919): Irish novelist and philosopher. *Sartre* (1954); *Under the Net* (1954); *Flight from the Enchanter* (1956); *The Sandcastle* (1957); *The Bell* (1958); *A Severed Head* (1961); *An Unofficial Rose* (1962); *The Unicorn* (1963); *The Italian Girl* (1964); *The Red and the Green* (1965); *A Time of Angels* (1966).

James Ngugi (b. 1938): Kenyan novelist. *Weep Not, Child* (1964); *The River Between* (1965); *A Grain of Wheat* (1967). Lives in England.

Edna O'Brien (b. 1932): Irish novelist and scriptwriter. *The Country Girls* (1960); *The Lonely Girl* (1962); *August Is a Wicked Month* (1965); *Casualties of Peace* (1966); film: *Girl with Green Eyes*.

C. Northcote Parkinson (b. 1909): English social and political historian and journalist. *Trade in the Eastern Seas* (1937); *War in the Eastern Seas* (1954); *Parkinson's Law* (1957); *Evolution of Political Thought* (1958); *The Law and the Profits* (1960); *British Intervention in Malaya* (1960); *In-Laws and Outlaws* (1962); *East and West* (1963); *Law Unto Themselves* (1966). Professor of History, University of Malaya, Singapore, 1950–58. Has traveled widely throughout Southeast Asia.

Roger Peyrefitte (b. 1907): French author and ex-diplomat. *Special Friendships* (1950); *Diplomatic Diversions* (1954); *Diplomatic Conclusions* (1954); *The Keys of Saint Peter* (1957); *The Knights of Malta* (1959); *The Exile of Capri* (1965); *The Prince's Person* (1965); *The Jews* (1967).

Harold Pinter (b. 1930): English playwright and scriptwriter. *The Caretaker*, and *The Dumbwaiter* (1961); *The Birthday Party*, and *The Room* (1961); *Three Plays* (1962); *The Homecoming* (1966); films: *The Servant; The Pumpkin Eater; Accident.*

William Plomer (b. S. Africa, 1903): English poet, novelist, and short story writer. *Turbott Wolfe* (1926); *The Case Is Altered* (1932); ed., *Kilvert's Diary* (3 v., 1938–40); *Double Lives* (1943); *Museum Pieces* (1952); three operatic libretti for Benjamin Britten (1953–66); *Collected Poems* (1960)

Anthony Powell (b. 1905): English novelist and critic. *Afternoon Men* (1931); *What's Become of Waring* (1939); *John Aubrey and His Friends* (1948); novel sequence, *The Music of Time*, of which the first volume was *A Question of Upbringing* (1951) and the eighth and latest, *The Soldier's Art* (1967).

J. B. Priestley (b. 1894): English novelist, dramatist, and critic. *The Good Companions* (1929); *Angel Pavement* (1930); *Dangerous Corner* (1932); *Time and the Conways* (1937); *I Have Been Here Before* (1938); *Johnson Over Jordan* (1939); *The Linden Tree* (1948); *Literature and Western Man* (1960); *Lost Empires* (1965); *Writings on Philosophy, Science, and Politics* (1965); *It's an Old Country* (1967).

D. N. Pritt (b. 1887): English barrister, author, and pamphleteer. *Light on Moscow* (1940); *Must the War Spread?* (1940); *The Labour Government, 1945–51* (1963); *Autobiography* (3 v., 1965–66). Labour Member of Parliament, 1935–40, Independent Labour, 1940–50. Professor of Law, University of Ghana, 1965–66; specialized as defense advocate in political cases in many countries.

James Purdy (b. 1923); American novelist and short story writer. *Color of Darkness* (1957); *Malcolm* (1959); *The Nephew* (1960); *Children Is All* (1962); *Cabot Wright Begins* (1964); *Eustace Chisholm and the Works* (1967).

Kathleen Raine (b. 1908): English poet and literary critic. *Collected Poems* (1956); *The Hollow Hill* (1965); *Collected Poems* (1966); in the press: *Blake and Tradition;* with G. M. Harper, *Thomas Taylor the Platonist; Defending Ancient Springs: Collected Essays.*

Frederic Raphael (b. 1931): American novelist, screenwriter, and critic. *The Earlsdon Way* (1958); *A Wild Surmise* (1961); *The Trouble With England* (1962); *Lindmann* (1964); *Orchestra and Beginners* (1967); films: *Nothing but the Best; Darling; Two for the Road.* Lives in England.

Simon Raven (b. 1927): English novelist. *Brother Cain* (1960); *Feather of Death* (1960); *Doctors Wear Scarlet* (1961); *Decline of the Gentleman* (1962); *Close of Play* (1962); a ten-volume novel sequence, *Alms for Oblivion,* of which the first volume was *The Rich Pay Later* (1964) and the latest, *Friends in Low Places* (1966).

Herbert Read (b. 1893): English poet and critic of literature and art. *The Meaning of Art* (1931); *Collected Essays* (1938); *Education Through Art* (1943); *The Philosophy of Modern Art* (1952); *Anarchy and Order* (1954); *The Contrary Experience* (1963); *Collected Poems* (1966).

Mary Renault: English-born novelist. *The Charioteer* (1953); *The Last of the Wine* (1956); *The King Must Die* (1958); *The Bull From the Sea* (1962); *The Mask of Apollo* (1966). Has lived in South Africa since 1948.

Kenneth Rexroth (b. 1905): American poet, editor, translator of poetry from Chinese, Japanese, Greek and Latin, and painter. *In What Hour* (1940); *The Phoenix and the Tortoise* (1944); *The Signature of All Things* (1949); *Thirty Spanish Poems of Love and Exile* (1955); *One Hundred Poems From the Japanese* (1955); *One Hundred Poems From the Chinese* (1956); *Thou Shalt Not Kill* (1956); *The Bird in the Bush* (1959); *Assays* (1961); *An Autobiographical Novel* (1966); *Collected Shorter Poems* (1967). One of America's first abstract painters.

David Riesman (b. 1909): American social scientist and essayist. *The Lonely Crowd* (1950); *Faces in the Crowd* (1952); *Individualism Reconsidered and Other Essays* (1954); *Constraint and Variety in American Education* (1956); *Abundance for What? and Other Essays* (1964). Henry Ford II Professor of Social Science, Harvard University. The present essay on Vietnam is drawn from the text of a speech delivered at a "speak-out" in Harvard Memorial Chapel, March 1966.

Alain Robbe-Grillet (b. 1922): French novelist, scriptwriter, and film maker. *The Voyeur* (1958); *Jealousy* (1959); *In the Labyrinth* (1959); *The Erasers* (1964); *For a New Novel* (1966); *La Maison des Rendez-vous* (1967); films: *L'Année Dernière à Marienbad; L'Immortel; Le Paris-Orient Express.*

Harold Rosenberg (b. 1906): American art critic and essayist. *The Tradition of the New* (1959); *Arshile Gorky: The Man, the Time, the Idea* (1962); *The Anxious Object: American Art and Its Audience* (1965). Art critic of *The New Yorker.*

Philip Roth (b. 1933): American short story writer and novelist. *Goodbye, Columbus* (1959); *Letting Go* (1962); *When She Was Good* (1967).

Richard H. Rovere (b. 1915): American historian and journalist. With A. M. Schlesinger, Jr., *The General and the President* (1951); *Affairs of State: The Eisenhower Years* (1956); *Senator Joe McCarthy* (1959); *The American Establishment* (1962); *The Goldwater Caper* (1965).

Bertrand Russell, 3rd Earl (b. 1872): English philosopher, mathematician, educationalist, and sociologist. With A. N. Whitehead, *Principia Mathematica* (3 v., 1910–13); *Introduction to Mathematical Philosophy* (1919); *The Practice and Theory of Bolshevism* (1920); *The Analysis of Mind* (1921); *The Analysis of Matter* (1927); *A History of Western Philosophy* (1945); *Human Knowledge: Its Scope and Limits* (1948); *Authority and the Individual* (1949); *Unpopular Essays* (1951); *Human Society in Ethics and Politics* (1954); *Nightmares of Eminent Persons* (1955); *Why I Am Not a Christian* (1957); *Common Sense and Nuclear Warfare* (1959); *Basic Writings of Bertrand Russell* (1961); *Fact and Fiction* (1962); *Has Man a Future?* (1962); *Unarmed Victory* (1963); *The Autobiography of Bertrand Russell* (1967); *War Crimes in Vietnam* (1967). In 1916 Russell was convicted and fined as the author of a leaflet criticizing a sentence of two years' hard labor passed on a conscientious objector. In 1918 he was sentenced to six months' imprisonment for writing a further article also judged subversive. Professor of Philosophy, Peking Government University, 1920–21. Has devoted much of the past 13 years to opposing the danger of nuclear war and the pursuit of the Cold War. Chairman of the Continuing Committee of the Pugwash Conferences on Science and World Affairs. Former President of the Campaign for Nuclear Disarmament and of the Committee of 100, organizations devoted to the cause of nuclear disarmament. Was sentenced to two months' imprisonment, later reduced to seven days, for refusing to be bound over to be of good behavior and keep the peace, the summons referring in particular to inciting the public to demonstrate against nuclear weapons. In November 1966 he convened an international tribunal on US war crimes in Vietnam. The first public hearings were held in Stockholm in May 1967. Awarded the Nobel Prize for Literature in 1950.

William Sansom (b. 1912): English novelist, short story writer, and essayist. *South* (1948); *The Body* (1949); *Among the Dahlias* (1957); *The Last Hours of Sandra Lee* (1961); *The Stories of William Sansom* (1963); *Away to It All* (1966).

Nathalie Sarraute (b. Russia, 1902): French novelist and critic. *Portrait of a Man Unknown* (1958); *Martereau* (1959); *The Planetarium* (1960); *The Age of Suspicion: Essays on the Novel* (1962); *The Golden Fruits* (1964).

Arthur M. Schlesinger, Jr. (b. 1917): American historian. *Orestes A. Brownson* (1938); *The Age of Jackson* (1945); *The Vital Center* (1949); with R. Rovere, *The General and the President* (1951); *The Age of Roosevelt* (3 v., 1957–   ); *A Thousand Days: John F. Kennedy in the White House* (1965); *The Bitter Heritage: Vietnam and American Democracy, 1941–66* (1967). Served during Second World War in US Office of War Information, Office of Strategic Services, and US Army. Professor of History at Harvard, 1947–61. Served as Special Assistant to Presidents Kennedy and Johnson, 1961–64. He is now Schweitzer Professor of the Humanities at the City University of New York.

Ramón Sender (b. 1902): Spanish novelist. *Earmarked for Hell* (1932); *Seven Red Sundays* (1935); *Counter-Attack in Spain* (1938); *Dark Wedding* (1943); *Chronicle of Dawn* (1944); *The King and the Queen* (1948); *The Affable Hangman* (1954); *Before Noon* (1957); *Exemplary Novels of Cibola* (1963). During the regime of Primo de Rivera he was imprisoned for his Republican activities, held without trial, and released only after intervention by the Press Association of Madrid. Throughout the Republic he remained highly critical and refused all office. When the Civil War began, he enlisted at once in defense of the Republic and served until 1938—finally commanding a brigade—when opposition from Communist elements forced him to leave Spain. He has lived in the US since 1942; naturalized in 1945. Currently Visiting Professor of Spanish Literature, University of Southern California, Los Angeles.

Irwin Shaw (b. 1913): American novelist, playwright, and short story writer. *Bury the Dead* (1936); *The Gentle People* (1939); *The Assassin* (1945); *An Act of Faith* (1946); *The Young Lions* (1948); *The Troubled Air* (1950); *Mixed Company* (1950); *Lucy Crown* (1956); *Tip on a Dead Jockey and other Stories* (1957); *Two Weeks in Another Town* (1959); *Voices of a Summer Day* (1965); *Love on a Dark Street* (1965). Has lived in Switzerland since 1956.

Konstantin Simonov (b. 1915): Russian poet, novelist, playwright, and journalist. *The Russians* (1943); *Days and Nights* (1944); *The Russian Question* (1946); *Comrades in Arms* (1953); *Victims and Heroes* (1963); *Soldiers Are Not Born* (1964). In 1939 Simonov was sent to the Far East to report the battle of Khalkhin Gol in Outer Mongolia. Throughout the Second World War he served as an army correspondent, reporting for *Red Star* and *Pravda* from almost all the Russian battlefronts. To the mass of Soviet people who lived through the 1941–45 war, he is probably best known for his war poem entitled "Wait for Me." Following the war he served as a Deputy in the USSR Supreme Soviet convocations of 1946 and 1950; Deputy, Russian Soviet Federative Socialist Republic Supreme Soviet Convocation of 1955; member of the Central Auditing Commission of the Communist Party of the USSR, 1956–61. Simonov was sharply criticized as an "individualist" for the poem "A Few More Days," the story "Pantaleev," the novel *The Quick and the Dead,* and other works which had appeared during the literary "thaw." In 1957 he was removed from the editorship of *Novy Mir* for publishing Dudintsev's novel *Not by Bread Alone* and other works. He was not present at the 1958 Constituent Congress of the RSFSR writers. In 1966 it was decided to publish the "hot" war memoirs of Simonov in the December issue of *Novy Mir.* These were critical of Stalin's leadership at a time when official policy was to desist from the attacks on Stalin begun by Khrushchev. Two members of the editorial board of *Novy Mir* were dismissed during the heated debate behind the scenes which led to the December issue being a month late, but were later reinstated after strong pressure from a number of writers. In the end Simonov's memoirs were not published because he refused to accept cuts in his manuscript.

C. P. Snow (b. 1905): English novelist. *The Search* (1934); *The Two Cultures: and a Second Look* (1963); an eleven-volume novel sequence, *Strangers and Brothers,* of which the first volume was *Strangers and Brothers* (1940) and the ninth and latest, *Corridors of Power* (1964). Created Life Peer, 1964; served as Parliamentary Secretary to the Ministry of Technology, 1964–66.

Edgar Snow (b. 1905): American sinologist. *Far Eastern Front* (1934); *Red Star Over China* (1937); *The Battle for Asia* (1941); *The Political Battle of Asia* (1941); *People on Our Side* (1944); *Pattern of Soviet Power* (1945); *Stalin Must Have Peace* (1947); *Journey to the Beginning* (1958); *The Other Side of the River* (1962). Has traveled extensively in the Orient and visited practically every country from Baluchistan to Siberia. Most of

his adult life has been spent in China, Japan, Manchuria, India, and the Dutch Indies. Currently writing a book about Mao Tse-tung, whom he first met in 1936 and last interviewed in 1965. Lives in Switzerland.

Susan Sontag (b. 1933): American novelist and critic. *The Benefactor* (1963); *Against Interpretation* (1966); *Death Kit* (1967).

Terry Southern (b. 1924): American novelist, short story writer, and critic. *Flash and Filigree* (1958); with M. Hoffenberg, *Candy* (1959); *The Magic Christian* (1960); ed., *Writers in Revolt* (1963); co-author of film scripts: *Dr. Strangelove; The Loved One.*

Stephen Spender (b. 1909): English poet and literary critic. *Poems* (1933); *Trial of a Judge* (1938); ed., with J. Lehmann, *Poems for Spain* (1939); *European Witness* (1946); *World Within World* (1951); *Collected Poems, 1928–53* (1955); *The Struggle of the Modern* (1963); *Worlds Within Worlds* (1966). Caught up in the political movement of the thirties, he published *Forward from Liberalism* (1937) and, shortly afterward, joined the Communist Party for a brief period. In 1937, he was the only British delegate to ignore the refusal of visas and attend the International Writers' Congress in Spain. He stayed in Spain for several months, in the midst of the Civil War, and one result was a number of translations of Spanish Loyalist poets. In 1948 he studied the impact of Nazism on German intellectuals for the Political Intelligence Branch of the Foreign Office. Spender records his total disillusionment with communism in *The God That Failed* (ed., R. H. S. Crossman, 1950). Consultant in Poetry in English to US Library of Congress, 1966. Following revelations, in May 1967, that *Encounter* had been financed by the Central Intelligence Agency, Spender resigned from the editorial board of the journal.

Enid Starkie: Irish biographer and literary critic. *Baudelaire* (1933); *Arthur Rimbaud* (1938); *André Gide* (1953); *From Gautier to Eliot* (1960). Reader Emeritus in French Literature at Oxford.

Christina Stead (b. 1902): Australian novelist. *The Salzburg Tales* (1934); *Seven Poor Men of Sydney* (1934); *House of All Nations* (1938); *The Man Who Loved Children* (1940); *Letty Fox, Her Luck* (1947); *Dark Places of the Heart* (1966). Lives in England.

George Steiner (b. 1929): American author and critic. *Tolstoy or Dostoevsky* (1959); *The Death of Tragedy* (1961); *Anno Domini* (1964); *Language and Silence* (1967). Lives in England.

I. F. Stone (b. 1907): American journalist, author, and editor. *Underground to Palestine* (1946); *The Hidden History of the Korean War* (1952); *The Truman Era* (1953); *The Haunted Fifties* (1963).

William Styron (b. 1925): American novelist. *Lie Down in Darkness* (1951); *The Long March* (1957); *Set This House on Fire* (1960); *The Confessions of Nat Turner* (1967).

Harvey Swados (b. 1920): American novelist, short story writer, and essayist. *Out Went the Candle* (1955); *On the Line* (1957); *False Coin* (1960); *Nights in the Gardens of Brooklyn* (1960); *A Radical's America* (1962); *Years of Conscience,* (1962); *The Will* (1963); *A Story for Teddy* (1965); *The American Writer and the Great Depression* (1966).

Philip Toynbee (b. 1916): English novelist and critic. *The Barricades* (1943); *The Fearful Choice: A Debate on Nuclear Policy* (1959); *Pantaloon* (1962); ed., *Underdogs* (1961); *Two Brothers* (1965); *A Learned City* (1965).

Barbara W. Tuchman (b. 1912): American historian and journalist. *The Lost British Policy* (1938); *Bible and Sword* (1956); *The Zimmermann Telegram* (1958); *The Guns of August* (1962); *The Proud Tower* (1966). Reported the Spanish Civil War from Madrid for *The Nation,* 1937. Editor on Far East news desk in the Office of War Information, New York, 1943–45.

Kenneth Tynan (b. 1927): English author and drama and film critic. *He That Plays the King* (1951); *Alec Guinness* (1953); *Bull Fever* (1955); *Curtains* (1961); *Tynan on Theatre* (1964). Literary Manager of the National Theatre.

John Updike (b. 1932): American novelist, poet, short story writer, and essayist. *Carpentered Hen* (1958); *The Poorhouse Fair* (1959); *The Same Door* (1959);

Rabbit, Run (1960); *Pigeon Feathers and Other Stories* (1962); *The Centaur* (1963); *Telephone Poles and Other Poems* (1963); *On the Farm* (1965); *Assorted Prose* (1965); *The Music School* (1966).

Gore Vidal (b. 1925): American novelist, playwright, and critic. *Williwaw* (1946); *The City and the Pillar* (1948); *Messiah* (1954); *A Visit to a Small Planet* (1957); *The Best Man* (1960); *Rocking the Boat* (1962); *Julian* (1964); *Washington, D. C.* (1967). Democratic-Liberal candidate for Congress, 1960.

Rex Warner (b. 1905): English novelist, poet, classicist, and translator. *The Professor* (1938); *The Aerodrome* (1941); *Why Was I Killed?* (1944); *The Cult of Power* (1946); *Greeks and Trojans* (1951); *Vengeance of the Gods* (1955); *Young Caesar* (1958); *Imperial Caesar* (1960); *Pericles the Athenian* (1963). Lives in the US.

Sylvia Townsend Warner (b. 1893): English novelist, short story writer, and poet. *Lolly Willowes* (1926); *Mr. Fortune's Maggot* (1927); *The Corner That Held Them* (1948); *The Flint Anchor* (1954); *Boxwood* (1960); *Spirit Roses* (1962); *Swans on an Autumn River* (1966).

Vernon Watkins (b. 1906): Welsh poet and translator of poetry from French, German and Italian. *The Death Bell: Poems and Ballads* (1954); ed., *Letters to Vernon Watkins From Dylan Thomas* (1957); *Cypress and Acacia* (1959); *Selected Poems* (1966). Gulbenkian Fellow in Poetry at the University of Swansea.

Alec Waugh (b. 1898): English novelist and travel writer. *The Loom of Youth* (1917); *Hot Countries* (1930); *Island in the Sun* (1956); *In Praise of Wine* (1959); *My Place in the Bazaar* (1961); *The Early Years of Alec Waugh* (1963); *The Mule on the Minaret* (1965).

Auberon Waugh (b. 1939): English novelist and journalist. *The Foxglove Saga* (1961); *Path of Dalliance* (1964); *Who Are the Violets Now?* (1966).

James Wellard (b. 1909): English-born novelist and writer on Africa. *Memoirs of a Cross-Eyed Man* (1956); *The Affair in Arcady* (1959); *A Sound of Trumpets* (1960); *The Great Sahara* (1965). American citizen; lives in England.

Arnold Wesker (b. 1932): English playwright. *Chicken Soup With Barley* (1959); *Roots* (1959); *I'm Talking About Jerusalem* (1960); *The Kitchen* (1961); *Chips With Everything* (1963); *Their Very Own and Golden City* (1964); *The Four Seasons* (1965). Wesker played a leading role in demonstrations against the use of nuclear weapons and, together with Bertrand Russell and other notable Englishmen, was sentenced to one month's imprisonment.

Richard Wilbur (b. 1921): American poet, translator, editor, and teacher. Trans., Molière's *The Misanthrope* (1955); *Poems, 1943–56* (1957); with Lillian Hellman, *Candide*, a comic opera (1957); ed., *The Complete Poems of Poe* (1959); *Advice to a Prophet* (1961); trans., Molière's *Tartuffe* (1963). Professor of English at Wesleyan University, Connecticut.

Angus Wilson (b. 1913): English novelist, short story writer, and critic. *The Wrong Set* (1949); *Such Darling Dodos* (1950); *Anglo-Saxon Attitudes* (1956); *A Bit Off the Map* (1957); *The Middle Age of Mrs. Eliot* (1959); *The Old Men at the Zoo* (1961); *Late Call* (1964); *Tempo: The Impact of Television on the Arts* (1966).

Colin Wilson (b. 1931): English essayist, novelist, and playwright. *The Outsider* (1956); *Religion and the Rebel* (1957); *Ritual in the Dark* (1960); *Beyond the Outsider* (1965); *Introduction to the New Existentialism* (1966); *Voyage to a Beginning: A Preliminary Autobiography* (1967).

Tom Wolfe (b. 1931): American journalist and humorist. *The Kandy-Kolored Tangerine-Flake Streamline Baby* (1965); *The Pump House Gang* (1967).

Leonard Woolf (b. 1880): English historian, political essayist, and editor. *The Village in the Jungle* (1913); *After the Deluge* (3 v., 1931–53); *Quack, Quack!* (1935); *Barbarians at the Gate* (1939); *Sowing* (1960); *Growing* (1961); *Beginning Again* (1964); *Downhill All the Way* (1967).

The 1937 Questionnaire

THE QUESTION

To the Writers and Poets of England, Scotland, Ireland and Wales

It is clear to many of us throughout the whole world that now, as certainly never before, we are determined or compelled, to takes sides. The equivocal attitude, the Ivory Tower, the paradoxical, the ironic detachment, will no longer do.

We have seen murder and destruction by Fascism in Italy, in Germany—the organisation there of social injustice and cultural death—and how revived, imperial Rome, abetted by international treachery, has conquered her place in the Abyssinian sun. The dark millions in the colonies are unavenged.

To-day the struggle is in Spain. To-morrow it may be in other countries—our own. But there are some who, despite the martyrdom of Durango and Guernica, the enduring agony of Madrid, of Bilbao, and Germany's shelling of Almeria, are still in doubt, or who aver that it is possible that Fascism may be what it proclaims it is: "the saviour of civilisation."

This is the question we are asking you:

Are you for, or against, the legal Government and the People of Republican Spain?
Are you for, or against, Franco and Fascism?

For it is impossible any longer to take no side.

Writers and Poets, we wish to print your answers. We wish the world to know what you, writers and poets, who are amongst the most sensitive instruments of a nation, feel.

Paris—June 1937

Signed:

Aragon	Nancy Cunard	Pablo Neruda
W. H. Auden	Brian Howard	Ramón Sender
José Bergamïn	Heinrich Mann	Stephen Spender
Jean Richard Bloch	Ivor Montagu	Tristan Tzara

Excerpts from *Authors Take Sides on the Spanish War*

Of the 149 answers to the 1937 questionnaire, nine of the more interesting ones are given below. Their tone is not altogether representative of that of the book in which they appeared, the book consisting, for the most part, of straightforward expressions of support for the Spanish Republic. These nine replies were reprinted on a page which accompanied the Vietnam questionnaire.

FOR THE GOVERNMENT

Samuel Beckett

¡UPTHEREPUBLIC!

Cyril Connolly

FASCISM IS THE FIRST PROCESS by which the cynical few exploit the idealism of the many, by violence and propaganda through the use of a dictator. Its aim is to maintain the status of the rich by using the poor to fight battles. This cannot be done until the whole nation is rendered both warlike and servile. Those who will not make soldiers are not required; those who are not required are eliminated. What we can learn from Spain is the order and extent of that elimination before the stultifying of the human race can proceed. Intellectuals come first, almost before women and children. It is impossible therefore to remain an intellectual and admire Fascism, for that is to admire the intellect's destruction, nor can one remain careless and indifferent. To ignore the present is to condone the future.

Alastair Crowley

DO WHAT THOU WILT shall be the whole of the Law.

Franco is a common murderer and pirate: should swing in chains at Execution Dock.

Mussolini, the secret assassin, possibly worse.

Hitler may prove a "prophet"; time will judge.

Love is the law, love under will.

Aldous Huxley

MY SYMPATHIES are, of course, with the Government side, especially the Anarchists; for Anarchism seems to me much more likely to lead to desirable social change than highly centralised, dictatorial Communism. As for "taking sides"—the choice, it seems to me, is no longer between two users of violence, two systems of dictatorship. Violence and dictatorship cannot produce peace and liberty; they can only produce the results of violence and dictatorship, results with which history has made us only too sickeningly familiar.

The choice now is between militarism and pacifism. To me, the necessity of pacifism seems absolutely clear.

Sean O'Casey

I AM, OF COURSE, FOR a phalanx unbreakable round those who think and work for all men, and I am with the determined faces firing at the steel-clad slug of Fascism from the smoke and flame of the barricades.

AGAINST THE GOVERNMENT

Arthur Machen

MR. ARTHUR MACHEN presents his compliments and begs to inform that he is, and always has been, entirely for General Franco.

Evelyn Waugh

I KNOW SPAIN ONLY AS A TOURIST and a reader of the newspapers. I am no more impressed by the "legality" of the Valencia Government than are English Communists by the legality of the Crown, Lords and Commons. I believe it was a bad Government, rapidly deteriorating. If I were a Spaniard I should be fighting for General Franco. As an Englishman I am not in the predicament of choosing between two evils. I am not a Fascist nor shall I become one unless it were the only alternative to Marxism. It is mischievous to suggest that such a choice is imminent.

NEUTRAL

T. S. Eliot

WHILE I AM NATURALLY SYMPATHETIC, I still feel convinced that it is best that at least a few men of letters should remain isolated; and take no part in these collective activities.

Ezra Pound

QUESTIONNAIRE AN ESCAPE MECHANISM for young fools who are too cowardly to think; too lazy to investigate the nature of money, its mode of issue, the control of such issue by the Banque de France and the stank of England. You are all had. Spain is an emotional luxury to a gang of sap-headed dilettantes.

4536